FROM STANSB

THE
BULL MARKET

How to Make a Fortune on the Biggest Stock Market Bubble in U.S. History and Escape With Your Wealth Intact, Long Before the Crash

BY DR. STEVE SJUGGERUD

PLUS 28 SECRETS OF A SUCCESSFUL INVESTOR

"You Don't Need a Lot of Money to Invest Wisely and Live Well"

STANSBERRY
RESEARCH

About Stansberry Research

Founded in 1999 and based out of Baltimore, Maryland, Stansberry Research is the largest independent source of financial insight in the world. It delivers unbiased investment advice to self-directed investors seeking an edge in a wide variety of sectors and market conditions.

Stansberry Research has nearly two dozen analysts and researchers – including former hedge-fund managers and buy-side financial experts. They produce a steady stream of timely research on value investing, income generation, resources, biotech, financials, short-selling, macroeconomic analysis, options trading, and more.

The company's unrelenting and uncompromised insight has made it one of the most respected and sought-after research organizations in the financial sector. It has nearly 200 employees operating in several offices in the U.S. plus one in Asia, and it serves 350,000 customers in more than 120 countries.

About the Author

Dr. Steve Sjuggerud

 Before joining Stansberry Research in 2001, Dr. Steve Sjuggerud worked as a stockbroker, vice president of a global mutual fund, and a hedge-fund manager.

Over his career, Steve has addressed dozens of financial conferences in the U.S. and around the world, including the New York Stock Exchange. He has also been quoted by the *Wall Street Journal, Barron's,* and the *Washington Post.*

At Stansberry Research, Steve is the editor of *True Wealth,* which focuses on safe, unique, alternative investments overlooked by Wall Street. He believes that you don't have to take big risks to make big returns. And he has proven this to be true time and time again.

He is also the editor of *True Wealth Systems,* which uses a powerful data system, something typically found only at hedge funds and Wall Street banks, to pinpoint the sectors most likely to return 100% or more.

In 2016, Steve launched *True Wealth China Opportunities* in which he shows readers the simplest – and best – ways to take advantage of the triple-digit opportunity he sees building in many of the most innovative Chinese stocks.

Steve is the lead contributor to Stansberry Research's free e-letter *DailyWealth.* He co-founded *Standup Journal,* a magazine for stand-up paddle surfing (which, he says, was really just a great excuse to spend time traveling and getting to know his ocean heroes). And he has worked closely with many leaders in the guitar industry, pushing the limits and developing new products for guitar players.

Table of Contents

The Wise Investor

– Introduction –

I've had just about every job you could have on Wall Street. I've been a stockbroker, vice president of a mutual fund, and president of a 250,000-student program called Investment University.

And 15 years ago, I quit my last "real job" – running a hedge fund.

When I left the institutional game, some of my closest friends couldn't believe I "gave it all up."

But I was sick of corporate America. I couldn't stand the meetings... the politics... the constant pressure to sell.

So I said "goodbye" and left to pursue one of my greatest passions: independent financial research.

You see, I wanted to produce something impossible to find on Wall Street...

Research free of hidden agendas and conflicts of interest.

So I launched a private investment group called *True Wealth*.

At the time, I had no idea how successful it would become.

But today, this little project has grown into a movement that connects tens of thousands of people around the world.

Week after week, hundreds of people join our group.

First and foremost in this book, I want to tell you a story. At first glance, it may seem a bit simple. But as you'll see, understanding this story could be the key to protecting your wealth and growing your retirement account – safely – in the turbulent months ahead...

I'll never forget the week of March 20, 2000.

That's when the Nasdaq "dot-com bubble" reached its peak.

So many people were making so much money, the last thing they wanted to do was sell. It seemed like hundreds – perhaps thousands – of new millionaires were being minted each month.

But at the time, I took the opposite approach and issued a warning to all who would listen:

We are at the peak of most likely the greatest financial mania that we will ever see in our lifetimes.

For most people, it was hard to believe this engine of wealth creation – the stock market – could grind to a halt. And that tech stocks could collapse by 75%. But that's precisely what happened.

The Nasdaq imploded... And millions of investors lost a huge chunk of their life savings.

Now, I fear, it's going to happen again.

We are smack in the middle of the greatest stock market bubble in history. And when it bursts – it will devastate millions of investors.

To make matters worse...

If you have been kicking yourself for sitting in cash since 2009 and you've missed out on this massive bull run, you are not alone.

Some of the smartest people I know – millionaires who are incredibly successful in their various fields – have made the same mistake.

But I want you to please, please pay close attention to what I am about to say. This is your last warning... your final chance...

You will NEVER see another opportunity like this again.

Not in this lifetime.

My research indicates this bull market is not over.

Right now, we're on the verge of a massive panic.

But not the kind of panic most people expect.

Long BEFORE stocks collapse... We will witness an event that will send the Dow soaring past 40,000... 50,000 – even higher – as people who have sat on the sidelines so far panic *into* the markets.

You may disagree with my prediction or believe this sort of outcome is impossible.

But as you'll see, it has all happened before. And not just once. It has happened dozens of times... in many countries around the globe.

Now for reasons I'll share in a minute, I believe it's happening again, right here in America.

And if you make the right decisions today, you could double – even quadruple – the size of your retirement account... and escape the inevitable crash.

I've gone to great lengths to present my findings in as few pages as possible to give you the key facts and perspective you need to understand what's happening and why.

I hope this message helps you make sense of the world in the turbulent months ahead. It's something you may refer to again and again – as we reach the peak of this incredible bubble and its ultimate crash.

Good investing,

Dr. Steve Sjuggerud
Baltimore, Maryland
April 2017

PART ONE

The Last Bull Market

– Chapter 1 –

A Dire Warning From the Past

For you to understand the magnitude of this moment...

I need to share with you a brief glimpse into the past.

As you'll see – the pattern that's playing out in the markets today is not at all unique.

Take a look at this chart...

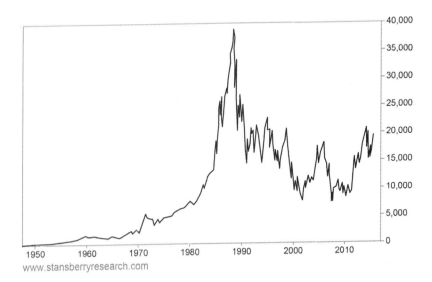

It's the stock index of one of the wealthiest nations in the world.

As you can see, it entered a furious bull market in the mid-1980s...

And investors who rode it higher had the chance to make a killing.

But then, the bubble burst.

And to make matters worse...

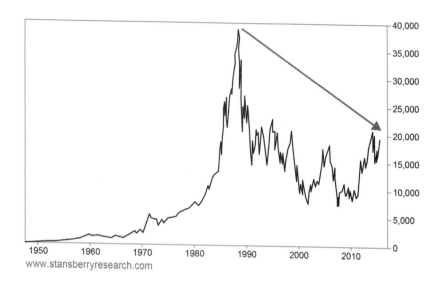

www.stansberryresearch.com

In 27 years, it NEVER recovered.

In other words, it was THE LAST BULL MARKET this country would ever see. Maybe they'll see another raging bull market someday...

But it's incredible... Almost 30 years later, these stocks are only worth HALF what they were worth at the 1989 peak!

Now, if you're a student of history, you may have guessed I'm talking about Japan.

At the time, it was said that the Japanese Imperial Palace was worth more than ALL the land in California.

Look at the chart again. Do you see how the Nikkei Index surged from around 5,000 to 40,000?

But pay special attention to this point, right here...

Nikkei Stock Market Index

www.stansberryresearch.com

Notice how a HUGE part of these gains came in the final year or two?

This final, furious stage of a bull market has a name... it's called a "Melt Up."

<u>And it's precisely what's happening in the U.S., right now</u>.

You might think Japan is a special case, but believe it or not...

The same exact thing happened right here in America, 100 years ago.

Back then, the United States' economy was booming. They called that era "The Roaring Twenties."

Dow Jones Industrial Average Index

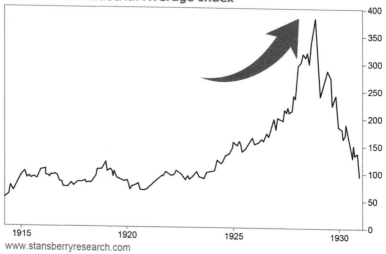

And you're probably familiar with the Great Depression that followed.

But most people don't realize – before the market crashed – the same pattern played out.

Take a look...

Between 1922 and 1929, the Dow Jones Index soared from 100 to almost 400.

Dow Jones Industrial Average Index

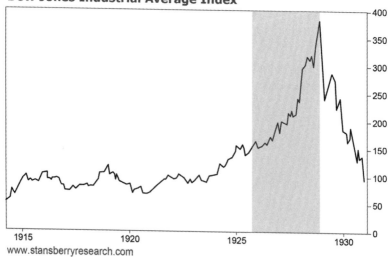

But the majority of these gains came in the FINAL year or so before the big crash. Can you spot the Melt Up?

For investors, it was a once-in-a-lifetime opportunity to get rich, almost overnight.

But after the bubble burst... it took 26 years to recover. And the average buy-and-hold investor never got back to "even."

At the time, the average life expectancy was just 53 years of age. So the typical investor over the age of 27 never lived to see the market recover. Thankfully, the average American today can expect to live well into their 70s. But the fact remains, if history repeats – the typical American over age 50 will NEVER see another bull market in his or her lifetime.

Dow Jones Industrial Average Index

26 years to get back to even...

And like I said – the incredible thing is, this is NOT an isolated pattern. You can trace it back to just about EVERY major bubble in history.

– Chapter 2 –

Why History's Greatest Mania Is About to Repeat

During the 17th century Dutch Tulip craze, the price of a single tulip bulb soared 30 times higher in less than two years.

Enough to grow every $10,000 into $300,000.

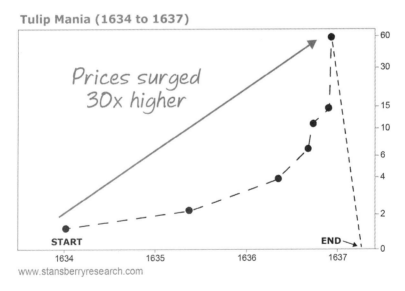

Tulip Mania (1634 to 1637)

Prices surged 30x higher

START
END
1634   1635   1636   1637

The same pattern appeared in 18th century France. Just imagine watching a $1,000 investment grow to $20,000 almost overnight.

That's what happened during the infamous Mississippi Bubble... French investors poured their money into a single firm – the Mississippi Company – which enjoyed a trade monopoly with France's North American colonies.

Mississippi Bubble (1719 to 1720)

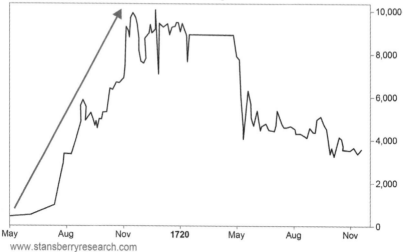

Incredibly – this single company obtained the right to mint new coinage and collect taxes on behalf of the government. And its rise triggered a fantastic bubble...

So many folks got rich, the French coined a new word to describe them... "millionaires."

And you might recall, the same thing happened during the Nasdaq bubble of the late 1990s.

NASDAQ Composite

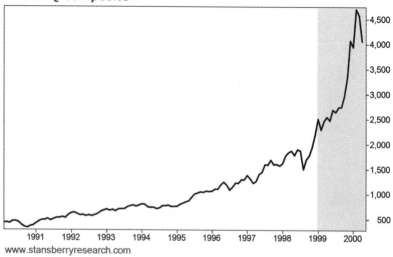

If you look back through history, you'll see all these manias and bubbles end the same way – with a furious Melt Up, then a final crash.

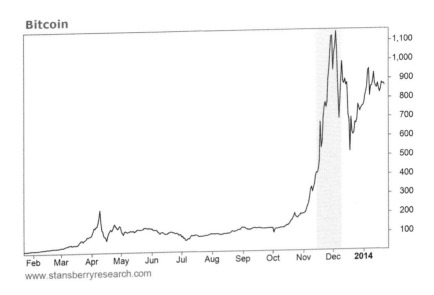

Bitcoin

Hong Kong Stock Market Index

Russian Stock Market Index

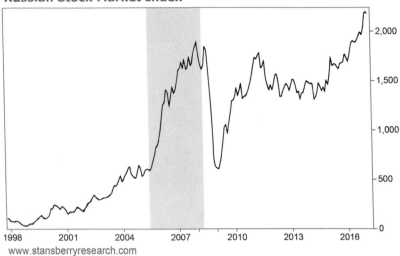

Platinum

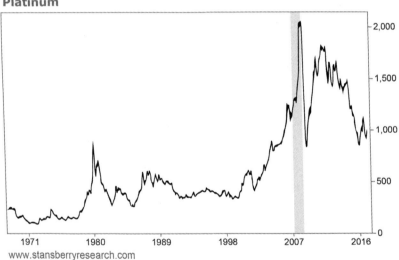

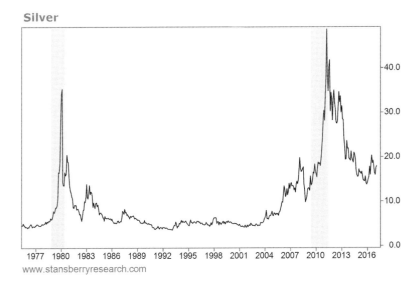

Silver

www.stansberryresearch.com

Which brings us to 2017.

The stock market has been rising for eight years...

A lot of folks think it can't run much higher.

They think it's up over the last several months because of the "Trump Bump."

But this is not how bull markets end.

Bull markets do not end when so much money is on the sidelines.

Bull markets end when everyone is invested... and there's no one left to buy. And that's precisely why they end... because with no one left to buy, prices have nowhere to go but down.

Remember back in 2005? People thought real estate was a one-way bet...

Everyone from hairdressers... to cabbies... to guys working the counter at McDonald's seemed to be buying and flipping houses.

That's a sign of a top.

And it's NOT at all what we're seeing today.

According to a recent Gallup survey, HALF of Americans don't own any stocks, at all.

And investors are sitting on record amounts of cash: $70 TRILLION, according to investment-management firm BlackRock.

According to National Geographic, 40% of Americans believe stocking up on supplies or building a bomb shelter is a wiser investment than a 401(k).

So if you're still afraid – haunted by the ghosts of 2008 – you are not alone. But once again, the masses are wrong and you must act fast, or you're going to miss out.

I know it may seem hard to believe.

Everywhere you look there seems to be "bad news."

The government is borrowing and printing trillions of dollars.

0% interest rates are strangling anyone living on a fixed income.

And everything from student loans... to the number of Americans on Food Stamps... to the national debt... are screaming "CRISIS AHEAD."

But despite all that...

You could (bare minimum) DOUBLE the size of your retirement account in the next 12-24 months.

If you buy a simple index fund, you'll probably do OK.

But if you want to capture the biggest gains... the kind that could turn every $100 invested into $500... $1,000 or more, you're going to have to do something completely different.

In the next few chapters, I'll show you exactly what to do.

But before we get to that, you might be wondering...

If we're on the verge of a stock market Melt Up... why is NO ONE talking about it?

Well, if you're a student of history – you can probably guess:

Both the mainstream press and average investors are almost always wrong.

– Chapter 3 –

How 'Fake News' Could Destroy Your Retirement

"Fake News" has gotten a lot of attention since the 2016 election cycle.

But I'm not going to discuss politics.

You see – beyond the issue of left vs. right is a far greater problem. The press does not exist to inform you. The press does not exist to protect your retirement or help you "get rich."

It's simply there to sell advertising. And to do so, it must make big, bombastic predictions – which are not based in fact.

If you don't do your homework... and if you take their predictions at "face value"... it could cost you everything.

For example...

Back in 1979 – *BusinessWeek* published an issue predicting "The Death of Equities."

Do you remember this cover? It was perhaps the worst stock market prediction in history.

All because of what happened next.

Over 10 years, the S&P 500 TRIPLED...

And individual stocks soared even higher:

- Circuit City went up 8,252%

- Hasbro soared 5,582%

- The GAP gained 3,694%

- Dillard's was up 3,817%

- Cooper Tire rocketed 2,081%

- Even plain old shares of Wal-Mart gained an incredible 4,032%

It happened again in 1988.

New York Times columnist, Paul Krugman, made a boneheaded prediction: The Internet will have no greater economic impact than the fax machine. Boy, was he wrong! The Internet boom, of course, minted *countless* new millionaires.

Here's another...

Recently, *The Economist* analyzed 220 forecasts from the International Monetary Fund (IMF). In 15 years, guess how many calls they got right?

ZERO!

I could go on...

It's hard to believe anyone trusts these so-called "gurus" anymore!

They couldn't see the crash of 2008 coming.

And what are they saying today?

This time, they're warning you to brace for a new stock market crash.

And once again, they're dead wrong!

We are in the final stages of a massive bull market. And the BIGGEST gains lie *ahead*.

Now I know, to most people, the financial world *seems* like a scary place.

And it is.

Government spending and debt are out of control.

Private corporations are borrowing trillions of dollars.

And according to Michael Hartnett – Chief Investment Strategist for Bank of America – investors have been hoarding cash at the highest levels since 2001.

It says so... right in this copy of his 2017 outlook. Take a look...

2017 Year Ahead Outlook — Bank of America Merrill Lynch

Investment Strategy
How are Cash Levels Changing?

Michael Hartnett
Chief Investment Strategist, BofA Merrill Lynch Global Research

QUESTION/STATEMENT: How are cash levels changing?

MR. HARTNETT: Throughout 2016 there have been a number of events: China, the oil price early in 2016, Brexit in the middle of 2016, and of course the U.S. election later on in the year that were event risks. They caused investors to hoard cash, and indeed coming into the U.S. election, we had the highest cash levels according to Bank of America Merrill Lynch surveys, that you had seen since 2001. That is now changing.

Cash levels are coming down as people are forced to buy equities. We would say a warning sign perhaps for this melt up that we're seeing right at this moment in asset markets would come if we started to see cash levels drop well below 5%. That would be a sign to us that euphoria was beginning and that would be a moment that we would go to our clients and say just be a little bit careful about anticipating too many gains from asset prices in the near term.

Can you imagine?

$70 trillion in cash that was sitting on the sidelines is now gushing into the stock market. And it's only just the beginning!

Out-of-control government spending... trillions of dollars sitting on the sidelines... and the Dow Jones Index soaring beyond 20,000 – to unthinkable heights.

You might think these trends are unrelated.

But as you'll see, there is an incredible connection between them. And if you understand this point... it could change your life.

Since last fall...

Billionaire investors and hedge funds have started diving into the market.

According to Merrill Lynch, "a whopping $63 billion poured into U.S. stock funds after Donald Trump won the presidency."

The *Wall Street Journal* called it "the biggest post-election rally ever."

Even the light-weights at CNN Money said it's "one of the biggest money flows of all time."

And stocks are beginning to go vertical.

The world's most "bearish" hedge fund, Horseman Capital, gave up... and began closing out its "short positions."

And now...

CNBC reports: "Panic is starting to set in about missing the rally."

This is it – the Melt Up has begun.

But the truth is – it has little to do with Donald Trump's election.

The seeds of this massive boom were planted years ago...

Back when I first predicted Dow 50,000.

At the time, few people believed me...

When I appeared on CNBC and Bloomberg News – the hosts looked at me like I was crazy.

Viewers weren't too kind, either...

They attacked my conclusion...

> *"Bad advice... Only a fool would get into the stock market at this point."*

Questioned my sanity...

> *"What an idiot!"*

And laughed me out of the room...

> *"LOL – Steve you are funny."*

Well, they're not laughing now!

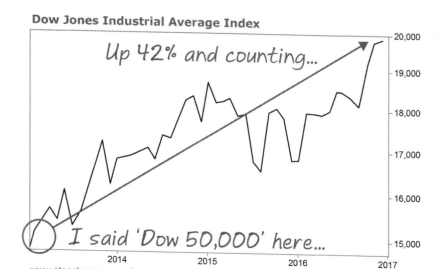

Dow Jones Industrial Average Index

Up 42% and counting...

I said 'Dow 50,000' here...

Because ever since my prediction, stocks have soared 42% as of early 2017.

But I don't blame the mainstream press and average investors for being wrong...

– Chapter 4 –

We Are Living Through an Unusual Time in History

Nothing seems to make sense.

Think about it...

Former President Barack Obama was awarded the Nobel Peace Prize – then proceeded to drop 26,172 bombs in 2016 alone!

The Federal Reserve printed $12 trillion out of thin air... Yet the dollar strengthened, considerably.

U.S. Dollar Index

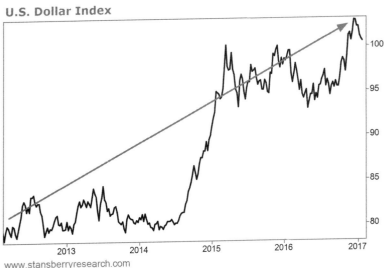

www.stansberryresearch.com

And perhaps most strange of all... the Chicago Cubs won the World Series.

But kidding aside... **this is your final warning**...

Obviously, I can't tell you how high stocks will soar. And like any investment... there's always a risk you'll time it wrong. Or lose money. There's sure to be a few bumps in the road and corrections along the way.

But my research points to one simple conclusion:

History is about to repeat itself.

We're entering the final stage of this epic bull market – a massive Melt Up.

Remember: The same thing happened back in 1920s America...

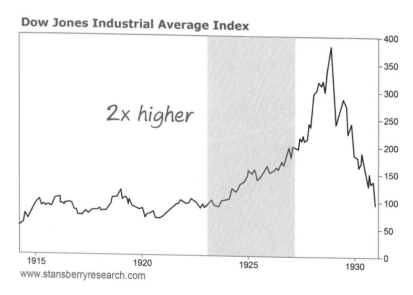

Dow Jones Industrial Average Index

2x higher

www.stansberryresearch.com

Stocks DOUBLED between October 1923 and October 1927.

Then, within two years – they doubled *again*.

Dow Jones Industrial Average Index

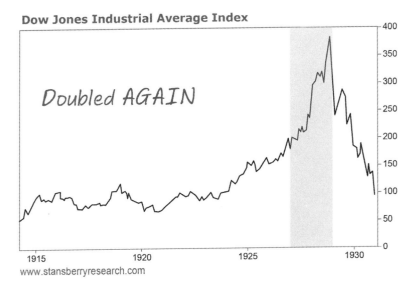

Doubled AGAIN

www.stansberryresearch.com

It happened in 1980s Japan...

Between 1978 and 1986, the Nikkei Index rose from just over 5,000 to more than 13,000.

Then came the final Melt Up. And stocks TRIPLED in value.

Nikkei Stock Market Index

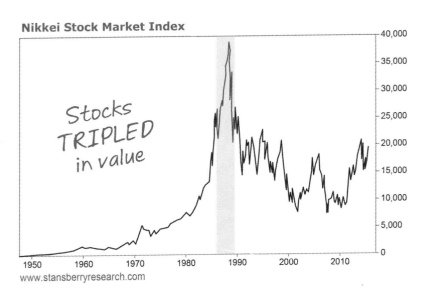

Stocks TRIPLED in value

www.stansberryresearch.com

And again, during the dot-com boom of the 1990s... Between late 1991 and 1996, the Nasdaq Composite doubled.

NASDAQ Composite

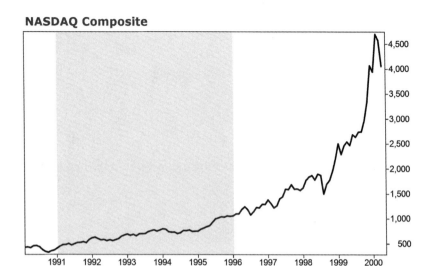

Was the rally over?

A lot of folks thought so.

But they were wrong.

In a final, furious Melt Up, stocks TRIPLED in the space of 18 months.

NASDAQ Composite

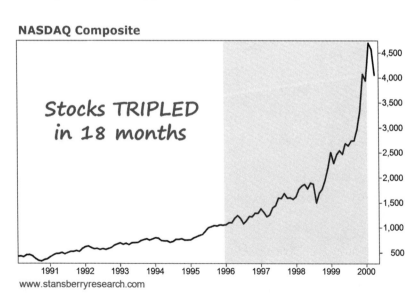

Now, the pattern is playing out again – with a twist.

You see – all the huge bull runs I've mentioned – from 1920s America to 1980s Japan to 1990s Nasdaq – were driven by the same speculative mania present today.

And to top it off...

There's something incredible happening today that has never occurred in 5,000 years of human history...

Never before have we seen a Melt Up start with interest rates THIS close to ZERO – and in some cases, negative.

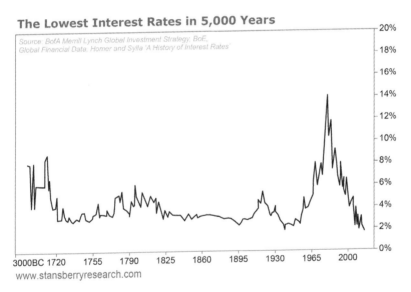

We know from experience – low interest rates are like rocket fuel.

And if you look all the way back to the age of Shakespeare... back to the Middle Ages... even before the birth of Christ... you won't see anything like this.

Most investors still have no idea what's going on.

They might be ignorant of world history... but they are not blind. And when they finally see what's happening... they're going to panic and pile into the stock market like never before. The whole thing will feed on itself. Week after week... stock prices will leap higher and higher.

If you think of the bull market since 2008 as a fireworks show... THIS is the grand finale.

The months to come will be one of the most spectacular things you've ever seen.

– Chapter 5 –

The Next 12 Months Could Change Your Life

Imagine waking up to find the size of your retirement account has doubled. Then you look and see it's all thanks to a small $500 investment.

I know it sounds impossible...

But during a Melt Up – this sort of thing can actually happen.

Take the most recent Melt Up for example...

Back in the 1990s, you could have put just $500 in stocks like...

- Dell
- EMC
- Best Buy
- Microsoft
- Charles Schwab
- Home Depot

Not penny stocks... We're talking household names.

And over the course of the

FROM HOUSEHOLD NAMES TO HUGE GAINS (1990S)

Company	Percent Gain
Dell	89,374%
EMC	80,238%
Best Buy	9,959%
Microsoft	9,566%
Charles Schwab	8,261%
Home Depot	3,698%

www.stansberryresearch.com

decade, $500 placed into each – a total investment of $3,000 – would have made you a millionaire.

To a lesser extent...

The same thing happened in 1980s Japan...

Sony soared 305%... Mitsubishi leapt 268%... and Nintendo surged 351%.

And in 1920s America...

I could show you dozens of examples...

But here's what I find fascinating:

The stock market rose so far and so fast, the number of millionaires counted by the U.S. Treasury multiplied from just 21 to an estimated 15,000.

Now it's going to happen again...

Tens of thousands of new millionaires could be minted in the months ahead.

But it's important you act right away, because a huge new investor is entering the market... And it's going to trigger a stock-buying panic... the likes of which you've never seen.

You might be wondering – who is this "mysterious investor" I'm talking about?

Here's a hint...

It's not the hedge funds or billionaires I mentioned a moment ago. And no, I'm not talking about mom-and-pop investors in America. Yes, those folks are all going to pile into this Melt Up too... but there's a tidal wave of money coming that's even bigger...

Someone *else* is going "all in."

And they're richer than Warren Buffett, Carl Icahn, and Bill Gates COMBINED.

I'm talking about the world's central banks.

BANK OF JAPAN

These institutions have an awesome power that no mortal could dream of: The power to print money.

Trillions of dollars – on demand.

But I'm not talking about the usual "stimulus" you've heard of before.

For the first time ever – central banks are now funneling trillions of dollars directly into the stock market.

As of early 2017, the Swiss National Bank owned MORE shares of Facebook than the social media company's founder, Mark Zuckerberg.

According to Bloomberg, the Bank of Japan is on track to be the No. 1 buyer of Japanese stocks. And if its buying binge continues – within a few years, it will own the ENTIRE market!

China's central bank is now a Top 10 shareholder in the biggest, most well-known stocks in Shanghai.

And the U.S. Federal Reserve has cracked the door open. Fed Chair Janet Yellen says, "There could be benefits to allowing the central bank to buy stocks."

If you think that's crazy... you're right.

It's totally nuts.

This has never happened before.

And according to a recent survey by Invesco, 80% of central banks plan to buy *even MORE* stocks in 2017!

The *Wall Street Journal* just published the results of its study... and they're incredible.

Do you see what's happening? They're pulling massive amounts of cash out of commercial banks... and plowing it into the stock market.

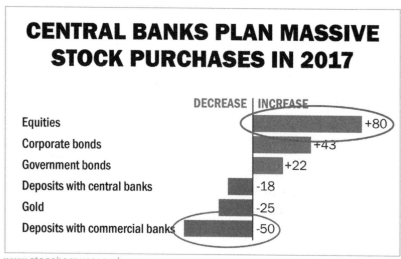

CENTRAL BANKS PLAN MASSIVE STOCK PURCHASES IN 2017

	DECREASE	INCREASE
Equities		+80
Corporate bonds		+43
Government bonds		+22
Deposits with central banks	-18	
Gold	-25	
Deposits with commercial banks	-50	

www.stansberryresearch.com

In other words...

Trillions of dollars in "funny money" is about to flood into stocks.

In 5,000 years of recorded history, this has never happened.

NEVER before have interest rates hit 0% (or negative).

NEVER before have central banks taken a direct, multitrillion-dollar stake in the stock market.

And not since 2001 have so many regular investors been sitting on the sidelines in cash...

Conditions are in place for the most spectacular stock market Melt Up in history!

In the coming months, this tidal wave of cash – trillions of dollars – will crash through one segment of the market... then another... and another.

And if you position yourself properly... you may never have to worry about money again.

How high could the market soar?

If the market Melts Up 109%, like it did during the Roaring Twenties, the Dow would top 41,000.

If it repeats the pattern we saw during the Nasdaq's Melt Up of the late 1990s, it would explode to 48,000.

And if the market were to leap an insane 228% like it did in 1980s Japan, the Dow could rise to 65,000.

Dow 65,000 might sound like a stretch.

But remember 2009...

Investors were terrified of stocks. They poured money into "safe" investments like Treasury bonds... while the mainstream press fanned fears of a new Depression.

Few could imagine the market would more than TRIPLE over the next eight years.

Yet that's precisely what happened.

If you bought a simple index fund in 2009 and held on, you would have done well...

But you would have completely missed out on the biggest gains on stocks like General Growth Properties, which soared 9,975% or Regeneron Pharmaceuticals, up 2,465%... or even household names like Netflix and CBS, both of which soared more than 1,500%.

General Growth Properties

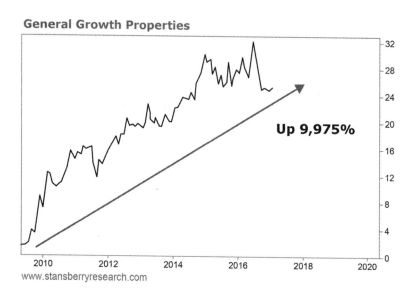

Up 9,975%

www.stansberryresearch.com

Regeneron Pharmaceuticals

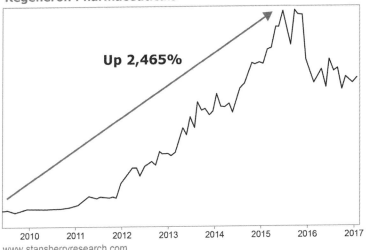

Up 2,465%

2010   2011   2012   2013   2014   2015   2016   2017

Netflix

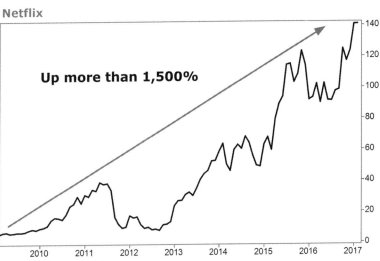

Up more than 1,500%

2010   2011   2012   2013   2014   2015   2016   2017

CBS, Corp.

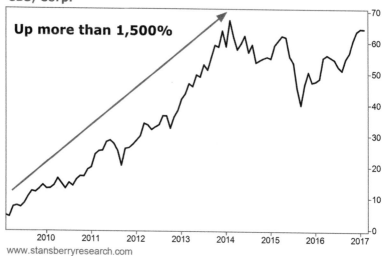

Up more than 1,500%

www.stansberryresearch.com

And now it's happening again...

But the lion's share of the profits won't be made on simple index funds or on stocks that soared over the past few years.

In fact, I'm not recommending you buy ANY stock listed on the S&P 500. There's a much, much better way to make money in the months to come.

Here's what I mean and why I'm making this recommendation so strongly...

– Chapter 6 –

The Greatest Melt Up in American History?

Not long ago, I was summoned to the headquarters of the New York Stock Exchange.

I was invited there by a famous billionaire... one of the wealthiest men in South America, whom I'm fortunate to call a close friend and mentor.

This man has lived through multiple bouts of hyperinflation and currency devaluation. And each time, he has emerged richer and more powerful than ever.

So I was flattered when he asked me to share my research with a small group of his wealthy friends and associates...

What were they after?

You see... ever since I launched *True Wealth* – I've developed a series of very successful "Investment Scripts," which help me figure out, like a game of chess, how to be a few moves ahead of the market and which stocks will show the biggest gains with the least amount of risk.

For example, I used a specific Script back in 2000 when I warned my readers to sell almost every position and wrote:

> We are at the peak of most likely the greatest financial mania that we will ever see in our lifetimes.

Sure enough, the Nasdaq fell more than 75%.

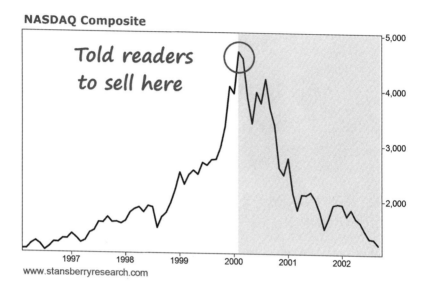

NASDAQ Composite

And again in 2002, I developed a Script for the housing boom that had just begun. I told my readers the No. 1 place to invest was the housing market... and that a real estate bubble would develop over the coming years.

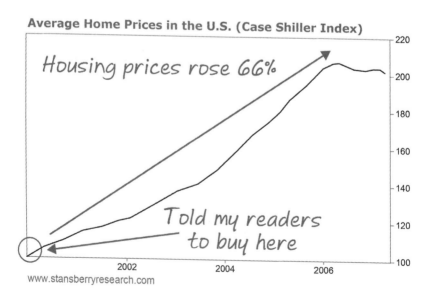

Average Home Prices in the U.S. (Case Shiller Index)

Those who listened and bought a house (or two) did well. The previous chart shows the average home price... which rose 66%.

And over the past several years, I tabbed several stocks anyone could buy through a brokerage account including...

D. R. Horton, Texas Pacific Land Trust, the Blackstone Group... and many more.

Housing Stocks	Percent Gain
D.R. Horton	96% (2004)
Beazer Homes	35% (2004)
Texas Pacific Land Trust	165% (2013)
Annaly Capital	17% (2013)
Two Harbors Investment	37% (2013)
Government Properties Income Trust	21% (2014)
Blackstone Group	192% (2015)
iShares U.S. Home Construction Fund	83% (2016)

Then in 2003, I developed a Script for what I thought would be a tremendous move in precious metals... which were just coming out of an extremely long bear market.

I told my readers, "The investment conclusion is simple, invest in gold."

Few analysts agreed. And the yellow metal was absolutely hated... trading for less than $400 an ounce.

But again, gold was precisely the right place to be.

Gold Price

It climbed all the way to $1,900 an ounce.

And the mining stocks we recommended soared even higher. One of my favorites, Seabridge Gold, went up 995%. That's enough to turn a single $10,000 investment into nearly $110,000. My Seabridge recommendation holds the No. 1 spot in Stansberry Research's Hall of Fame (a list of the Top 10 highest-returning closed positions in my publisher's history).

Seabridge Gold

Up 995%

You get the point. For all these big market moves, I developed very successful Scripts, which helped my readers see precisely where the market was going... and gave them the chance to reap the biggest gains.

And this brings me to my latest and perhaps most successful Investment Script.

I first caught onto it back in 2008, when the United States' central bank – The Federal Reserve – began printing money and lowering interest rates like we've never seen before.

So far, the Script has played out exactly how I predicted.

I've heard from folks who've literally made millions by following my research.

And now we're entering the final chapter...

A "violent rotation" is taking place.

More and more investors are waking up... and plowing their money into the stock market.

The mainstream media – the same folks who told you "Trump can't possibly win" and then "if he wins the markets will crash" – have been proven dead wrong.

Stocks are soaring.

But if you run out and buy the biggest winners of the past few years... you will be very disappointed.

There's a danger to what I've shared with you so far...

It's human nature to take the path of least resistance...

So you *might* be tempted to hold on to all your investments... or load up on shares of an index fund.

Why not? If the Dow is going all the way to 50,000 (or more), can't you just sit tight and ride it higher?

Not exactly...

Like I said before – if you're over age 50, this could be the LAST bull market you ever see.

It will likely be followed by a massive crash that will throw stocks... currencies... perhaps the entire financial system into chaos.

We could face DECADES of slow growth or no growth at all.

That's why your actions today are so important...

This is your last chance to build a retirement war chest that could last you all the way through the coming crisis.

And to do that, you'll want to do more than just double your money to protect yourself when the market finally collapses... currencies go haywire... and bond prices plummet.

More specifically...

You want to own the stocks that could exceed the simple stock market's return by a wide margin.

Most people won't recognize these investments until it's too late.

– Chapter 7 –

The Millionaire's Investing Script for 2017

As I mentioned... for years I've had a working Script for investing...

And I have one unspoken goal with the Script – to zero in on the ONE THING that matters most at that moment.

Fortunately, we've gotten it right for many years.

Our *True Wealth* Script can change as the facts (and investor perceptions) change. But since 2009, our core investing Script has been simple...

The Fed will keep interest rates lower than you think, for longer than you can imagine. And that will cause asset prices (like stocks and real estate) to soar higher than you can imagine.

Our Script for 2017 is that the Fed will raise short-term interest rates only a little bit – to about 1% by the end of 2017. That is not nearly enough of a hike in interest rates to derail the boom in asset prices.

Again, this is the same Script I've had for years. But that's because the "big picture" hasn't changed much.

What has changed is that the Melt Up is now beginning. And that means we want to be particularly aggressive. But the overall theme of betting on higher prices for stocks and real estate remains the same.

Plenty of things could derail this Script for 2017... Trump could unnecessarily and foolishly escalate tensions with China... or the economy could grow quickly, causing the Federal Reserve to raise interest rates dramatically... But we are assuming those things won't happen.

Interest rates will stay lower than you think for longer than you can imagine, and asset prices will soar higher than you can imagine. That's the view from 30,000 feet – but it doesn't give us the specifics.

So let's get down into the trenches and size up each major asset class through the lens of our Script to decide where to put our money in 2017.

We'll start with U.S. stocks...

U.S. STOCKS
New highs today... And more new highs to come in 2017

"I remember when the Dow hit 1,000, and then 2,000," a friend in his 70s told me at lunch. "Now the Dow's near 20,000. That's scary."

This friend is no dummy... He founded a major corporation that traded on the stock market. He had tens of thousands of employees. His net worth hit nine figures.

And he's scared.

I get that... We're in uncharted territory.

If prices hit a new all-time high, they only have two potential places to go... somewhere they've already been, or somewhere they've never been.

Our brains tell us stocks are more likely to fall... to a place they've already been before. That feels comfortable. That has already happened, at least.

It has to be a more likely outcome, right?

Our brains are wrong.

We have decades of data to prove it...

The truth is, new highs are a good thing for stocks.

I looked at what history says happens after stocks hit new 12-month highs. The surprising thing is that they continue moving higher...

You REALLY want to own stocks after a new 12-month high. And you really DON'T want to buy stocks after a new 12-month low.

The table below shows it best. It has the data going all the way back to 1928. Take a look...

Since 1928	12-Month Return	% of Time
After 12-month high	7.3%	31%
After 12-month low	2.8%	11%
No new high or low	4.4%	57%
All periods	5.1%	100%

S&P 500 compounded annual gains.
Based on monthly data, not including dividends.

These results are hard to believe. They go against what makes intuitive sense. But they aren't lying...

Stocks perform much better after new 12-month highs than they do after new 12-month lows.

We want to own stocks when they're hitting new highs... And they're hitting new highs right now!

Importantly, the Melt Up will likely keep pushing stocks higher. That could create a cycle of higher highs. It sounds crazy. But it's what I expect in 2017.

This is a story most folks don't understand or don't want to hear. But stocks have just hit new highs... That tells me they can have another strong year in 2017.

Shifting gears a bit... The other major "bear case" for stocks is something we've heard about for years...

"Stocks are too expensive. They can't continue higher from today's inflated prices."

But think with me for a second... What is one of the main drivers in our Script? **It's ultra-low interest rates**.

Investors have a choice today – between earning no interest in the bank, or taking risks in stocks.

Investors are *always* making that choice between earning safe interest somewhere or taking a risk in the stock market.

So to understand if stocks are a good deal, you have to consider whether they're a good deal relative to interest rates.

Said another way: You must consider both stock valuations AND interest rates when sizing up the value in stocks.

This is exactly why I built one of my favorite indicators: The *True Wealth* Value Indicator.

This simple value measure combines a stock's valuation – the price-to-earnings (P/E) ratio (adjusted for recessions) – with short-term interest rates.

P/E ratio + short-term interest rate = True Wealth Value Indicator

Short-term interest rates contain a lot of information about the investing environment. Inflation is part of short-term interest rates. And so are the actions of the Federal Reserve.

So our *True Wealth* Value Indicator tells us a lot. As you can see from the next chart, stocks were incredibly cheap at the bottom in 2009... And they were extremely expensive at the top in 2000. This indicator works.

Right now, we're about in the middle of the range... Stock valuations are not high compared with our indicator's history. Take a look...

True Wealth **Value Indicator**

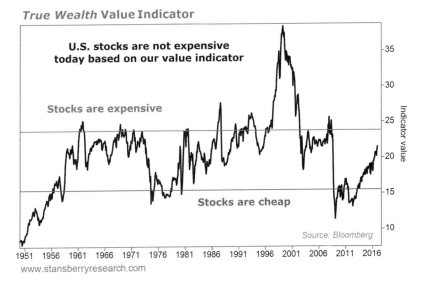

Most people think stocks are expensive. But when you take today's ultra-low interest rates into account, you see that stock prices could easily go much higher from here.

Stocks would need to roughly double to hit the valuation highs they reached during the last Melt Up in the late 1990s. So while it might sound crazy, it's completely possible from here.

So we have two important factors in play right now...

1. Stocks are hitting new highs, which is good going forward, and

2. Stocks are NOT expensive relative to history when you add in interest rates.

In short, more new highs are likely in the stock market in 2017. The Melt Up is already starting. And there's every reason to expect big gains from here.

History tells us that stocks could double from here, like they have in previous Melt Ups. But there's actually a simple way to dramatically increase those returns.

Here are the details...

The Simple Way to Double the Return on Stocks During the Melt Up

Few investors realize it, but there's a simple way to double your potential returns in stocks.

It's easy... You don't to have to use options or anything like that. You can make the investment in any normal brokerage account.

You don't have to take big risks either. You can limit your downside like you would with any investment. So your chances of "going to zero" are no larger than with a normal stock investment.

What's great is that this kind of investment is perfect for the Melt Up.

Remember, the Melt Up is likely going to lift all stocks higher. There will be winners and losers, of course. But the overall market could double, based on history.

That means owning the entire market is a great idea. But we can do even better...

We can own the entire market with a single click and end up with roughly double the overall return during the Melt Up.

How do we do it? With one of my favorite kind of investments... leveraged ETFs.

A leveraged ETF might sound exotic and scary at first. But it's a simple concept...

ETF stands for exchange-traded fund. They're funds that hold a basket of assets, usually stocks.

The SPDR S&P 500 Fund (SPY) is the world's largest ETF. All it does is hold the stocks in the S&P 500. Instead of owning the S&P 500 through a mutual fund, you can own it with an ETF through SPY.

I often recommend ETFs in *True Wealth* because they offer simple ways to make big-picture bets.

And when we really believe in an idea, I often look for *leveraged* ETFs to capitalize on it.

These leveraged ETFs work like you'd expect. They allow you to own a certain basket of stocks, but with two or three times leverage.

Say you expect the health care sector to move higher in price. You could take advantage of this with a normal health care ETF. But if you have conviction in your idea, you could take a bit more risk and invest with leverage.

You could easily make the trade with the ProShares Ultra Health Care Fund (RXL). This fund returns twice the daily change of the U.S. health care sector.

If health care stocks go up 1% today, RXL should go up by about 2%. But if health care stocks fall by 1%, RXL will fall by about 2%, too.

The important thing to remember here is that leveraged ETFs work on a daily basis. They don't promise to return a consistent leveraged result over a long period.

Consider the chart below. It shows shares of RXL versus the overall health care sector from 2010 through 2014. Take a look...

Leveraged Health Care vs. Regular Health Care

Health care stocks were up by nearly 150% over this five-year period. And they consistently moved higher, as the chart shows.

Because of this continued "up" action, owning leveraged health care – with RXL – led to much better returns... around 400% gains.

You see, because health care stocks moved higher and higher without a breather, the leverage compounded over a few years. So the long-term gain became much more than double what the health care sector produced.

This is a fantastic feature when stocks are moving higher. And that's exactly what we expect to happen during the Melt Up.

The Melt Up will cause stocks to move higher... potentially doubling in the next few years. And that means owning them through a leveraged ETF could lead to double that return... or more.

Remember, SPY from earlier? It's the simplest way to own the S&P 500 with an ETF. Well there's a leveraged version of SPY… the ProShares Ultra S&P 500 Fund (SSO).

SSO returns twice the daily gain or loss of the S&P 500. So if stocks double over the next few years, SSO could easily lead to 200% gains. And as the health care example earlier shows, the returns could be even higher than that!

Now, SSO isn't an official *True Wealth* recommendation today. But it and other leveraged ETFs will be great tools to profit during the Melt Up. And I'll let you know the exact time to put these tools to work in your portfolio.

Now that we've covered the big ideas in the U.S. market, let's look at a couple other important asset classes. Starting with real estate…

REAL ESTATE
Don't wait another second: Buy!

Get to Florida and buy a house. Now.

The median home value in Orlando, Florida is around $164,200, according to Zillow.com. The median home value in Jacksonville, Florida is $147,400.

I can't tell you that the median home in these places is the right home for you, but my point is that Florida real estate is still CHEAP. When I travel the world, I'm stunned by the prices…

When I was in Shanghai and Beijing in 2016, I learned that a small apartment (that you wouldn't want to live in) costs over a million dollars. And in Vancouver in the summer of 2016, I learned that nearly all houses in the city are over a million dollars (in Canadian dollars).

Compared with Shanghai and Vancouver, they're practically giving away houses in Florida.

Meanwhile, there's *no* supply of homes in Florida...

Homebuilding in Florida has been below the trend for a very long time now. Take a look...

Florida New Private Housing Building Permits

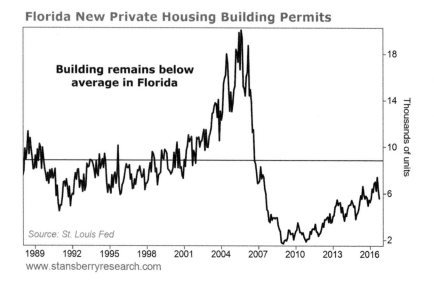

One of the basic rules of economics is that prices rise when there's no supply of something that's in demand. Without enough supply, house prices should rise in Florida.

Florida real estate has so many things going for it... including a warm climate, no state income taxes, and typically lots of elbow room (compared to a cramped Manhattan apartment, for example). Meanwhile, because prices are so low, you can still earn a good yield by renting out a property.

And think about this...

You can bet that the Trump administration – run by a real estate mogul – will be extremely friendly toward real estate owners and investors. Plus, mortgage rates are still not far from all-time lows. It is a perfect setup.

I'm practicing what I'm preaching here...

With my own money, my largest asset class is Florida real estate – not stocks, bonds, or anything else. (And that excludes my home.)

Florida is just one example... Much of America's real estate is CHEAP.

It won't stay this way forever. I expect U.S. real estate to perform well during the Melt Up. And I believe now is a fantastic time to buy a home or other real estate if you're in the market.

Again, this is where the majority of my investments are today. So I've put my money where my mouth is. I suggest you do the same.

Now, you understand the best ways I see to profit in the U.S. during the Melt Up. But there's one more idea I need to share with you...

– Chapter 8 –

How to Get Out Before the Crash

We know it's coming...

We know that the Melt Up will lead to a massive boom in U.S. stock prices. But we also know what will happen next...

A major bust... one that could take decades to recover from.

I'm not trying to scare you. Remember, we've seen this before, time and time again... in the U.S. and other markets.

When a Melt Up ends, a big crash usually follows. And while we're taking advantage of the Melt Up today, we have to understand how to protect ourselves when the bust begins.

This chapter will show you exactly how I plan to do that.

You see, we have a simple strategy to protect our gains. I've recommended it for years... I think you'll see that it's a foolproof way to protect yourself in the post-Melt Up crash.

Don't Lose Money:
The Most Important Law of Lasting Wealth

Buying stocks is easy. There are thousands of theories out there on why and when to buy. But buying is only the first half of the equation when it comes to making money.

Nobody ever talks about the hard part – knowing when to sell.

Let's face it – most people don't know when to sell a falling stock.

They're frozen into inactivity, saying, "Should I just keep holding and hoping, or should I cut my losses now?" This state of indecision is usually permanent and often continues until you hear this: *"Well, it's too late to sell now."*

But if you follow an exit strategy, your constant state of indecision will be gone. You'll never lose another night's sleep worrying about which way your investments will go tomorrow. Unlike most investors, you'll have a plan – knowing when to get out and when to stay in for the biggest possible profits.

We've all made expensive mistakes – either missing the full upside by selling too soon or taking a huge loss by holding a falling stock too long. But it's time to make big losses a thing of the past.

To invest successfully, you need to put as much thought into planning your exit strategy as you put into the research that motivates you to buy the investment in the first place.

The Trailing Stop Strategy

In stocks, you must have and use an exit strategy – one that methodically makes you cut your losers and let your winners ride.

If you follow this rule, you have the best chance of outperforming the markets. If you don't, your retirement may be in trouble.

The exit strategy I advocate for is simple. I ride my stocks as high as I can... But if they head for a crash, I have my exit strategy in place. That protects me from damage.

Though I have many levels of defense and many reasons I could sell a stock, if my reasons don't appear before the crash, the trailing stop strategy is my last-ditch measure. I use it to save my hard-earned dollars. And it works.

The main element to the trailing stop strategy is a 25% rule. I will sell any and all positions if they fall 25% off their highs.

For example – if I buy a stock at $50 and it rises to $100, I will sell it if it closes below $75 – no matter what.

The "no matter what" part is important. It doesn't matter how we feel about the investment. We can always make up reasons why the market is wrong and we're right. But when we hit a stop, the market is sending a clear signal: You're wrong. It's time to move on.

This is about being disciplined as investors. Using a trailing stop as a failsafe takes our emotions out of it. When we hit a stop, we sell. No questions asked.

That's the only way to protect ourselves from a portfolio-crushing mistake...

Don't Let Your Losers Become Big Losers

How did 2008 feel for your portfolio?

Most people think they can stomach a big fall. But when it actually happens, they panic.

They also believe they'll be willing to wait it out... and get back to even.

But when the time for "waiting" comes, they get impatient and sell.

That is the main reason we use fixed stops – stops that force us out no matter how we feel. They protect us from ourselves.

What's so magical about the 25% number? Nothing in particular. It's the discipline that matters.

Many professional traders actually use much tighter stops – the *Investor's Business Daily* newspaper, for example, recommends an 8% stop.

Ultimately, the point is you never want to be in the position where a stock has fallen by 50% or more. A 50% fall would mean that stock has to rise by 100% or more just to get back to where it was.

YOU'LL NEVER RECOVER

% Fall in Share Price	% Gain Required to Get Back to Even
10%	11%
20%	25%
25%	33%
50%	100%
75%	300%
90%	900%

By using this trailing-stop strategy, chances are you'll never be in this position again.

I must admit – it took me three years to truly follow my own advice on this one. I would always come up with some excuse for why I should keep holding dud stocks. Nearly every time with those losers, if I had practiced what I preached, I'd have been better off.

Now I always cut my losses. Once you get into the habit and commit to doing it, it is not hard.

One thing in life is certain: The future is uncertain.

Nobody – not even the most astute analyst or investment adviser – can know enough about a particular company, industry, or the nuances of the market to anticipate future price with 100% certainty.

But common sense dictates two fundamentals:

1. Taking small losses is much better than taking big losses, and

2. Letting your profits run is much better than cutting them off prematurely.

I recommend using end-of-day prices for your calculations, not intraday prices. This makes things easier. If a stock has gone to $100, put at least a mental stop at $75. If the stock closes at or below that $75 level, sell your shares the next day.

I do this because we think that **PLACING ACTUAL STOP ORDERS IS A BAD IDEA**. I do not recommend placing stop orders with your broker at all.

The dirty NYSE traders will be able to see the stop orders you place with your broker. They will pile up all the stop orders and then execute them all at a horrible price. Interestingly, stocks often close higher the very same day, after the NYSE traders make a mint executing stop orders. DON'T put a stop order in the market.

Simply sell the day after you hit your stop.

This is simplest way to follow trailing stops. Set a mental trailing stop and use closing prices.

We use a more advanced technique in *True Wealth*.

Don't worry. It's still simple for you to follow. But it has a better long-term track record than a simple 25% trailing stop.

My good friend Dr. Richard Smith developed this technique. And I've been recommending it to my *True Wealth* subscribers for years.

PART TWO

Secrets of a Successful Investor

You Don't Need a Lot of Money to Invest Wisely and Live Well

– How to Live Richly and Invest Wisely –

I hope you take advantage of the opportunity I've outline in this book.

We are smack in the middle of one of the biggest stock market Melt Ups in history.

But this time, it's going to dwarf what we saw in the Roaring Twenties… in 1980s Japan… and even the massive Nasdaq bubble of the late 1990s.

Without a doubt, this could be the LAST bull market you will ever see. And before it's over, stocks will soar higher and further than most people can imagine.

Follow the steps I've laid out in this book and you may never have to worry about money again.

Perhaps the most important lesson I can teach you along the way is…

You don't need a lot of money to invest wisely and live well. You simply have to keep wealth – as much or as little of it as you have – in perspective.

In Part Two of this book, we share 28 secrets of a successful investor. This is a compilation of some essays I've written over the years on how to live richly and invest wisely. Many of these are common-sense techniques that people tend to ignore on their blind search for ever-accumulating wealth.

You don't need to be rich to live richly. You just need to be smart...

As you read through the following essays, please keep in mind that any dates or numbers may no longer be relevant.
But the lessons are timeless.

THE RICH LIFE

Chapter 1

The No. 1 Secret to Wealthy Living

Published August 15, 2008

I'm living well.

The great thing is, "living well" by my definition doesn't cost much money at all. That's because my definition of living well isn't about, well, "stuff." Let me explain…

At the Oregon coast yesterday, I windsurfed perfect head-high waves alongside 2004 World Champion Scott McKercher. The day before, I went surfing with champion paddle surfer Ekolu Kalama and his wife. No crowd, just us.

For comparison, if you're a golfer, that's like hanging out with Tiger Woods for the day, just the two of you.

I feel fortunate to be here with these guys… and it reminds me of what's important in life:

It's about EXPERIENCE, not STUFF.

My wife and I try to live this idea – that "experience" is more important than "stuff."

For example, our kids (ages seven and five) are probably the only kids they know that don't have a PlayStation or an Xbox or a Nintendo Wii. They don't have a ton of **stuff**. But they've got a ton of life **experience**…

Our kids have seen the world... They've been as far north as Iceland. And they've been as far south as New Zealand. Yet we don't have big flat-screen TVs in our living room or den. (Are we the last Americans to actually have regular TVs?)

The great thing is, life experiences don't have to cost much at all. Waves are free. Wind is free. Spending time with your friends and family is free.

Before I came out to Oregon for vacation, we spent time with my family in Orlando. Over the weekend, the kids shot water guns at their granddad in the pool, and my mom fixed unbeatable home-cooked breakfasts. Everyone had a great time. It was a great family experience. And it sure didn't cost much. It's not what it costs that makes it valuable.

It wasn't about buying "stuff." And this trip to the Oregon coast isn't about "stuff" either.

I define living well as...

1. Having time with friends and family

2. Pursuing my passions, and

3. Not worrying about money.

The nice thing is, you don't need a fortune to live well by that definition.

Living well to me isn't about monster flat-screen TVs, driving a BMW, or wearing diamond-encrusted watches. How about you?

You only have so much money... so what do you put a premium on? It's so easy in America to be sucked into "stuff" – from the pressure to "keep up with the Joneses" to the constant barrage of advertising from every angle.

But you can't take stuff with you. I've heard investor Doug Casey say, "I've never seen a hearse with luggage racks." And if stuff is what you choose, just remember, you'll be busy working for the rest of your life to pay for your stuff.

If you follow my definition of living well, the goal becomes living life to the fullest instead of buying stuff... and saving instead of buying so you don't have to worry about money.

People want to invest successfully so they don't have to worry about money. **If you change your definition of living well**, **you can get to the point of not worrying about money a lot faster**.

Again, my idea of living well is..

1. Having time with friends and family.

2. Pursuing my passions (which I'm doing on the Oregon coast now).

3. Not worrying about money.

What's your idea of living well? Is it about the experience or the stuff?

Chapter 2

How to Retire With No Savings

Published November 27, 2011

"Do you have any savings?" I asked my friend Tony this week.

"Not really, no," he answered.

Tony is in his 50s. And he didn't sound worried in the least. How is that possible? I was surprised Tony was so relaxed...

My wife, for example, couldn't consider living like that. My wife is hardwired to save instead of spend. She really doesn't spend. And even though we have saved and invested well... she STILL worries.

Tony quit his job five years ago. And then he sold off a good deal of his possessions to finance living his dream.

Tony now builds extremely fine guitars. He has earned critical acclaim. He's doing what he always wanted to do. And he intends to do it for the rest of his life.

I visited Tony in Indiana. I came to visit so he could help me build my own guitar...

"This is my retirement," Tony said, pointing his arms around his shop.

"The Larson Brothers built guitars until they died in their 70s," he reminded me. "And John D'Angelico and Jimmy D'Aquisto built guitars until they died, too." Tony intends to do like these legends did.

In 2006, he had a "good" job as a computer graphic artist. And before that, he worked as a cabinetmaker. But making cabinets or pushing a computer mouse were not what he wanted to do with his life.

Guitars were always his passion. He'd been building and tinkering with them since the 1980s. So he took the leap. If it didn't work, he figured, he could sell off the contents of his guitar workshop and return to being a graphic artist.

I am not as bold as Tony. But I do admire him for following his passion.

He took what must have seemed like an enormous risk. But five years later, he's able to say something most people will never be able to say: He's living his dream, doing what he wants to for a living.

Tony has "retired" with basically no savings. And yet he is happy because he has set up the rest of his life to do what he loves.

Is following your dream worth a shot? Can you turn that into a way to make money? If it doesn't work, do you have something to fall back on? You only live once... Think about it.

– Chapter 3 –

You Can Escape This Market

Published March 10, 2009

You have to make some major changes in your life, right now. Fortunately, making those changes doesn't have to hurt…

My friend Grant Pecoff made big changes in his life. He and his wife Layne used to live in San Diego. They had a three-bedroom house, three cars, and every modern convenience. But he got tired of trying to keep up.

He realized he didn't need all that *stuff*.

Today, the Pecoffs have a one-bedroom house. And they share one car. But their quality of life is outstanding… and they're much happier. They're living on the water, on the island of Eleuthera in the Bahamas. My wife and I visited them over the weekend.

"A lot of people don't realize that **you can choose your life**," Grant told me.

"We realized that we had lost our priorities along the way. So we got out of San Diego to reconnect with what's important to us. It's a lot less stressful here in the Bahamas, and I get a lot more work done."

Grant is an artist. He lives in the Bahamas, but he still has his gallery in San Diego. Other galleries feature his art as well, like the Wyland Gallery in Key West (where I first saw his work).

While life as an artist might sound glamorous, it's stressful. Just think about it... Mortgage payments and car payments are fixed, but art sales vary. Your income goes up and down. So Grant did the smart thing.

He got rid of his old fixed payments.

Grant told me taking that initial leap and moving was huge. "That initial leap gave us the confidence to take more steps – to make more choices. When you think about it, the definition of 'leap' is that there is some moment where both feet are off the ground."

He told me, "Here, you can choose to never put shoes on all day... or to shower outside naked... or to walk for hours on the beach. It's up to you. We don't have fancy restaurants here or a hundred channels on TV. But they're not important to us."

The Pecoffs' new lifestyle is not for everyone... The house sits on a point, with water on two sides. But when they bought it, it had no electricity or running water. Even now, if you want a hot shower, you have to wait until the afternoon, when the sun has heated the water pipes on the roof. There's no air conditioning... You have to rely on the sea breezes. When it gets too hot, you take a dip in the ocean.

A Grant Pecoff original. To read his story and see more of his work, visit www.pecoff.com.

Grant's life is different than it was in San Diego. He made the leap. He made wholesale changes. He got rid of the anxiety. He got rid of the need to keep up with the neighbors.

If you're stressing right now about money, you ought to consider making some changes. With Grant as an example, the changes you make don't necessarily have to hurt as bad as you might think.

Grant escaped this market. He went down from three bedrooms to one... and from three cars to one. If you want to remove the anxiety, if you want to improve your quality of life, consider following Grant's lead.

You don't have to move to the Bahamas or go without electricity. But keep Grant's words in mind: "**You can choose your life**."

Take a moment to reflect on your priorities and see if you're living by them. If you're not, consider what changes you should make. Then... Leap!

Chapter 4

A Big Lesson From Scott's Hard Trade

Published January 20, 2010

I've done well since March 2009... A few of my accounts are up by triple digits in percentage terms.

But my returns are nothing compared with what my friend Scott did in the last two years...

Earlier this week, my wife and I met up with Scott and his wife for drinks. We made a point to tell Scott how impressive the trade he made was.

Let me tell you Scott's story...

In 2007, during the heyday of real estate, Scott was a big-shot mortgage broker for a major bank. He was the boss... He had a team of mortgage brokers under him.

Scott probably made a whole lot of money. He built a stunning custom home right on the water and had a deep-water dock for his fancy boat.

Everybody was flying high at the time... On the northeast coast of Florida, nearly everyone who got "rich" made their money from real estate somehow. They were investors, developers, builders, lenders... something. In the wealth race, even the doctors and lawyers got left behind by the guys in real estate.

But right around the peak in Florida real estate, Scott ended up losing his job.

What happened to the rest of the real estate guys when the music stopped? For just about all of them, they acted like the music was still playing.

What else were they going to do? Accept reality? No way...

Reality would mean taking a loss... So they held on and hoped. Few of the developers or builders were smart enough to get out at the top. Small paper losses turned into huge paper losses. They still hung on. They preferred to sink with the ship, hoping these once-in-a-lifetime days would return.

Not Scott... He was not "fooled by randomness." He didn't assume the once-in-a-lifetime real estate boom days would return. He didn't confuse genius with a bull market. Through either humility or brilliance (or both), Scott made a dramatic change in his life...

Scott made the hard trade.

When he lost his job, he immediately put his new fancy home up for sale. At a time when everyone around him was living extremely high on the hog, Scott downsized dramatically, buying a significantly smaller inland home – all in cash.

Scott hit the reset button.

He hit the button early. He didn't let his ego or his old high status get in the way. Instead, he started over, regardless of what the "country club" crowd thought.

Scott is now back at work, doing what he knows well... He's a mortgage broker again for a major bank.

"How's business?" I asked him when we met for drinks.

"Well, I'm not making any money. But I don't have a mortgage anymore either."

I complimented him on his bold life decision to downsize dramatically at the height of the boom. He said...

> Well, we just got back to what was important... We decided
> that STUFF wasn't that important. And stressing over STUFF
> is wasted energy. Our family is what's important. We made
> the big change, and life is much different. But it's good. Now,
> for the first time in my career, I'm able to see my kids at night
> when I get home from work.

Scott seemed just fine with the whole thing. He's not lying awake at
night, wondering how he's going to pay the mortgage.

Scott made the hard trade. He cut his losses early. The worst thing you
can do is hold and hope that yesterday will return. Are you lying awake at
night stressing about STUFF?

You can get out of it. You can follow in Scott's footsteps. You can hit
the reset button and start over at a much lower level of spending. You
can sell the fancy house and rent instead. You can sell the fancy car, or
boat, or whatever is keeping you up at night. It's all just stuff.

Sure, I had a decent year in my trades. But my trades pale in
comparison with Scott's bold trade... Scott traded stuff for happiness.
In his case, the bolder the downsizing, the greater the happiness.

If you're unhappy, if you're stuck holding and hoping, follow Scott's
lead. Trade your stuff for peace of mind and happiness.

Chapter 5

How Bill Beat Cancer

Published January 16, 2010

"Hey, Bill, it's GREAT to see you," I said. "How's it going?"

"Fantastic, Steve. What's new with you?"

We were bumping into each other in the doorway of our favorite breakfast joint earlier this week.

"Who cares what's new with me," I thought... BILL JUST BEAT CANCER. The thing is, I KNEW he would beat it...

The doctors might have told Bill he wouldn't make it. But those doctors couldn't have known who they were dealing with.

The doctors didn't know the Bill I know.

Bill has changed my life for the better – many times. If you follow his example, you can change your life for the better. And you can change the lives of the people around you, too. It's simple really, as I'll show you.

First, let me give you just two ways Bill improved my life...

In 2008, at the same breakfast joint, Bill was at another table. "Hey, Bill, you're looking great," I said. "What's your secret?"

"Thanks, Steve. I'm down 45 pounds AND I'm stronger than ever. I just got fed up with how I was living. So I decided to change. I started working out with this trainer named Fred. Steve, you've GOT to give this guy a call..."

Uh oh. I knew what was coming. Bill can sell me on anything. His positivity and enthusiasm is infectious. Bill sold me on Fred. I've been training with him for two years now. And I'm fitter than I've been since high school.

(When I got started, Fred told me how Bill tried his absolute hardest every day in the gym – with a smile. I'd see Bill working like an ox, literally – strapped into a harness, attached to a rope, dragging heavy stuff across the gym floor. Fred told Bill what to do to get strong... But Bill worked harder than anyone. It's Bill who got the results.)

For the second example of how Bill changed my life for the better... In short, Bill fixed my bad back. No, I don't mean Bill's a doctor. I mean he kick-started the process that led to my back being better.

One day, Bill invited me to do some sport. (I don't remember what it was.) I declined because my back was bothering me, and I didn't want to risk it.

"Ah, Steve, you should do what I do..."

Uh oh. I knew it was coming again. I knew Bill would sell me on something.

Bill had nothing personally to gain from these recommendations. Whatever Bill recommended, I knew it would ultimately be a good thing for me. And I knew if I did what he suggested with a fraction of the enthusiasm Bill has, I would be better off.

Bill told me...

> Steve, my dad died in his 40s. I didn't want to follow in his footsteps. So when I hit my 40s, I started doing a yearly 'executive physical' at the Mayo Clinic in Jacksonville. Even if you're healthy today, you ought to do it. It'll give you a benchmark of your health going forward. And they can address what's wrong now. Best thing I ever did.

I took Bill's advice. I did it... Best thing I ever did. The folks at Mayo eased all my little nagging concerns. And most importantly, they figured my back out. My back now feels better than it has in at least 10 years.

So my back is great... And I'm fitter than ever, working out with Fred twice a week. I give Bill the credit. These two things started not because of my initiative, but because I didn't want to let my friend Bill down.

So I was shocked to hear Bill was in the hospital a couple months ago. It was leukemia, and the doctors told Bill he may have waited too long. But Bill set a goal to be back in the gym with Fred before the end of 2009.

On the last day of 2009, Bill got to the gym with Fred. He's now home and he's getting back into shape.

By the way, Bill is an extremely successful businessman as well. I'm certain he'd be extraordinary at whatever he wanted to do.

And I think Bill's formula for extraordinary success in life – which has led him beat great odds on a regular basis – is easy to copy.

You don't need to be brilliant. Bill's formula doesn't require smarts. But you do need to do two things...

When he sets his mind to something, Bill will **work harder** than anyone to make it happen.

And Bill can summon a **positive attitude and incredible willpower** for long periods of time. In short, he convinces himself he can do it, no matter what "it" is.

I know, it sounds cliché... "Hard work and a positive attitude? That's all you've got, Sjuggerud?"

But think about it: Hard work and a positive attitude made Bill a multimillionaire and helped whip his life-threatening cancer. And Bill's infectious personality led me to fix my bad back and make me fitter than I've been since high school.

Your education, who you know, a bit of luck, how smart you are... these things will take you a certain distance in life. But if you want to be a huge success, there are no two ways around it. Fortunately, the formula is easy.

Work hard and stay positive that you will succeed no matter what.

In short, be like Bill.

– Chapter 6 –

If You're So Rich, Why Do You Still Work?

Published December 23, 2015

I have a few friends who have "silly" wealth – more wealth than they could ever need or spend.

These guys are at retirement age or older. But for some reason, they work harder than just about anyone else I know...

Why are they working so hard? Isn't the dream to "bank" enough money so you don't have to work?

I called a few of these friends over the years and asked why. The answers were interesting...

One wealthy friend started out with this story to explain it...

> I had dinner with an extremely wealthy guy who's 71. He just retired to the desert in Palm Springs, supposedly to play some golf. I asked him how it was going...
>
> "Retirement is horrible," he told me. He said, "I do NOT enjoy sitting in the desert doing nothing. I don't have a clue what I'm doing out here. I don't think I can do this. I don't need the money... But I think I'll have to go back to work."

My wealthy friend described the same feeling... "I love what I do," my friend told me. "I don't want to stop."

I asked my friends specifically what it is that keeps them working so hard...

One said, "Nothing in life beats the thrill of coming up with a big idea and making it a reality."

Another said, "I like mentoring younger people... passing on what I do and seeing them succeed at it."

A few more talked about the thrill of a great opportunity and the chance to increase their wealth. "I know there's no economic reason for me to work," one friend told me... "But that doesn't mean I don't like to get paid."

I then asked these friends if they had any advice to help people join them in the "big leagues"...

First, they explained, opportunity doesn't knock. You have to create it. And when opportunity is close by, you have to drop everything and pursue it. The more you make those sacrifices, the better your chances of finding financial success.

Second, if you KNOW MORE than everyone in the room, nobody can take advantage of you... So read a lot. Do more homework than anyone else at the table.

Finally, one friend told me, "Work to the task, not to the reward." Don't wash a car for the $5 payment, for example... Wash a car because that's the task at hand – and do a fantastic job. Then you'll get noticed for your work and have a chance to move up in the world.

So why do these "silly rich" guys still work? And how can you get there, too?

They work because they say it keeps them "alive..."

"If I stop working, I'll die," one of them told me. They believe that finding success is all about recognizing, creating, and seizing opportunities.

You make your own luck, they say, so create opportunities for yourself as best as you can.

If you do that enough times in life, you'll know you're giving yourself a legitimate shot at success... at having the kind of wealth that means you're working because you love to, like my friends, not working because you have to.

– Chapter 7 –

A Crazy Story... How You Can Avoid Getting Sucked In

Published April 30, 2013

"I can say with honesty that I have not contemplated taking my own life due to debt," a friend with big debts told me in an e-mail yesterday.

My friend's comment was about a crazy story...

Another man I know took his own life. Money worries are likely the main reason.

Apparently the guy who took his own life owed lots of people lots of money... The dollar amount totaled in the millions, I'm sure.

He's the second person I know this year that took his own life... for the same reason – money.

"Debt is a debilitating feeling," my friend with big debts continued. *"I am carrying a high enough stress level that I find it difficult to sleep at night."*

I lent this friend some money to help him get his business off the ground. But his business has hit unforeseen roadblocks. There is no cash flow yet. His money worries are real.

My friend is not alone...

Everyone has money worries. Everyone tosses and turns at night (at least a bit) about money.

The concern is when that "normal" worry crosses over into a dangerous worry… when you reach the point where you're in so deep, there is no getting out.

This mostly comes from getting in over your head with DEBT.

Most people don't see it coming. You think you're doing the right things, trying to get ahead in life. You see borrowing money as the way to get ahead. But the thing is, the debt remains, even if the plan doesn't work out.

The only advice if you're in that situation is to not throw good money after bad… Don't dig the hole deeper in order to get out. But the more important lesson today is: **Never let yourself get so indebted that your money worries consume your life**.

If you're an overachiever, this is hard to do… It's hard to play smart for the whole game of life, when temptation often shows its face. It's hard to play smart when you see an opportunity that is just above your reach… but could become a reality if you take on a lot of debt.

When you're dreaming about the big opportunity in front of you, all you think about is your upside potential – about how much money you'll make or how good you'll feel when all goes right.

But things do go wrong. Whether it works out or not… The debt remains.

Most people think it's normal to borrow a lot of money to start a restaurant or some other business… or to borrow money to speculate on a real estate deal or other investment.

Just because people think it's normal doesn't mean it's right. And I don't have the right answer for your situation. I don't know what the correct amount of debt is for you.

Except for taking a mortgage to buy a house… I think that if you don't have the money, don't spend the money.

Most people don't live by that standard. **But that standard will keep you out of trouble**.

You can live life with a clear head. And you will sleep soundly at night.

– Chapter 8 –

How to Be Dramatically More Productive, Successful, and Wealthy

Published December 22, 2015

A few years ago, I was out to dinner with a couple of the most successful guys I know – and they were giving me a hard time.

They were ribbing me about what Porter Stansberry calls the "Sjuggerud Advantage."

Hey, I can take it... The Sjuggerud Advantage, as I'll explain, is a major secret to my life's success.

Anyone can do it... The Sjuggerud Advantage requires no special skills. Let me tell the story...

We were at the Prime 112 restaurant in Miami Beach. It's a hip restaurant today, no doubt. As we were leaving, rap star Rick Ross was stepping out of his Rolls Royce and walking in.

Dinner was great... But my definition of a great dinner is "good times with good friends." I don't need a fancy bottle of wine or an unpronounceable delicacy to enjoy a meal.

Around 9:45 p.m., I started checking my watch... And Porter and the other guys at dinner gave me a bit of a hard time...

You see, I don't drink. I don't normally go out for fancy, three-hour meals. And most importantly, I go to bed early and get up early.

Porter was giving me a hard time about missing out on some of life's finer things. But I know these are parts of what Porter calls "the Sjuggerud Advantage."

I've heard Porter tell others: "You don't see the benefits of the Sjuggerud Advantage across a day or two. But over time, it adds up. *The guy gets a lot done.*"

It might sound silly. But I think the most important part of the Sjuggerud Advantage is simply getting out of bed... and doing it an hour earlier than anyone else...

"Getting to work early is such a common virtue of successful people that I'm tempted to call it the single most important thing you can do to change your life," my friend Michael Masterson wrote in his book *Automatic Wealth*. Michael's a self-made multimillionaire.

And I agree with him...

I get more done in the first two hours of my morning than I do in any other four-hour stretch during the day. More importantly, I get my BEST work done then – with no interruptions and no distractions, just focus.

I probably take it too far... I've come to *like* driving the streets when they're empty, before the sun has come up. I think it's partly because I know I'm going to get A LOT done.

And I've found that once it gets past 10:00 or 10:30 at night, I'm not very productive at all. I'm tired, I'm sidetracked thinking about the day's problems, and I'm better off calling it a day and starting up fresh in the morning.

While Porter would likely tell you there's more to it, I think simply getting up early is the big secret of the Sjuggerud Advantage. It's the big secret to getting a lot done.

It requires no special skills to get up a half-hour or an hour earlier than you usually do. And most of the extremely successful people I know get their days started very early. It's a simple thing, but it could have a dramatic effect over time.

As Porter said, you might not see the benefits after a day or two... But they add up. You get a lot more done early in the morning. And ultimately, you become more successful than the next guy.

It costs you nothing, and it could make you dramatically more productive, successful, and wealthy.

It has worked for me. I think it's the biggest part of the Sjuggerud Advantage.

It's so simple. But most people don't do it. Based on what I've described, though, isn't it at least worth giving it a shot?

– Chapter 9 –

The Best Advice for Success I Can Possibly Give You

April 17, 2017

I couldn't believe my good luck... I was going to be at a dinner with legendary investor Jim Rogers!

This was in 1996. I was 25 years old. Jim was a hero to me – he'd put together possibly the greatest track record of any living investor running a hedge fund in the 1970s.

I'd read his books, and he shaped a lot of how I think about the markets. So I was looking forward to meeting him in person for the first time. The dinner, and the investment conference it was part of, seemed like a great opportunity.

But my spirits sank as I walked in the room...

Twenty people were already seated at the dinner table.

I assumed many of those folks would want to get close to Jim... Maybe I wouldn't even be able to hear a few words from him. A handshake might be about it.

I scanned the table for empty seats. There weren't many. My buddy Porter Stansberry was with me. (He was 24 at the time.) I saw two empty seats together... And I couldn't believe it – these two empty seats were the two seats next to Jim Rogers!

All kinds of thoughts went through my head about why I shouldn't sit next to him:

- "Jim's a legend, and I'm a nobody. I don't deserve the seat next to him."

- "What if I say something foolish?"

- I'm supposed to be an expert like him, but what if he sees that I'm nobody special?"

Jim was a legend. I'm sure many of the other folks at the dinner had the same thoughts in their heads – and that's why none of them were sitting next to him.

I summoned my courage, put all those negative thoughts aside, and went for it...

Porter and I took a seat next to him. And it was one of the highlights of our lives to that point...

Jim couldn't have been more entertaining or charming for the next two-and-a-half hours... sharing his strong opinions on everything under the sun.

He knew that I knew a lot of details about his story. (For example, I knew his home phone number growing up in Demopolis, Alabama was "5." Not 555-5555. Just "5.") He was comfortable holding court – just for Porter and me. It was fantastic.

Since then, Porter and I have done a lot with Jim. He's been a speaker on our podcasts and conferences, and we don't hesitate to help each other out. And it all started because Porter and I faced our fears, took a chance, and simply sat down next to him.

To me, this is a secret to much of my success in life... Just getting past the fear of looking foolish, and taking the risk. It's hard to do... but it's the right thing to do.

This came up again recently... And I wanted to share the story with you...

Porter and I are no longer the young bucks we were in 1996. I will be 46 years old in a couple months. And our little business, Stansberry Research, has grown into a much bigger business.

Just recently, we had a couple-day meeting with many of our employees in Kiawah Island, South Carolina. One night at dinner, Porter and I sat at a table. The entire table filled up – except the two seats between us.

I asked Porter if he remembered the Jim Rogers dinner 20 years ago. He said, "Of course."

We wondered which young bucks would take the two empty seats between us. All the tables filled up... everyone took a seat... and the two seats between us stayed empty – for the entire dinner.

It was an opportunity wasted.

I'm sure the same things that were going through my head before we took a seat with Jim were going through people's heads in our company.

But trust me, you've got to step up. The upside is exponentially greater than the downside risk. Take the risk, and it can change your life for the better. Don't take the risk, and you're right where you were before the dinner – no worse off... but no better off.

I get that it seems like a big deal... and that it's tough to overcome your nerves. Back at that Jim Rogers dinner, many of the other folks in the room were successful legends in their own right... But even so, they were too intimidated to take those seats next to Jim.

Taking a seat at the table is just one way to follow today's advice...

Most people don't want to risk looking stupid. But I've learned that it's OK to say, "I'm sorry, I don't understand your idea. Can you explain it again?"

Jim Rogers didn't look at us like we were stupid. Instead, he appreciated that we were engaged in his ideas... wanting to understand them, wanting to learn more.

Again, I approach it the same way I approach investing... You want to accept a little bit of downside risk for a lot of upside.

In situations like this, the "math" is almost always the same – the potential upside is dramatically greater than the risk of looking foolish. You just have to overcome your fear of embarrassment.

Be bold, my friend. Summon your courage. Overcome your fears. Go ahead and take that seat at the (metaphorical) table. And potentially change your life.

You will be glad you did!

– Chapter 10 –

How to Become Friends
With Your Heroes

Published November 27, 2012

"You're so _lucky_ Steve... you've gotten to meet and work with all these famous guys..."

When I hear that, I usually say something like, *"Yeah, it's hard to believe... I have been pretty fortunate!"* and I leave it at that.

But the truth is much different... It's NOT luck. It's NOT good fortune. There's a secret to doing what I've done. And I will share it with you today... Maybe there is a bit of "luck" involved... But it didn't happen without me putting myself in luck's "line of fire." Let me give you an example of what I mean...

A while back, I knew I was going to have the chance to shake hands with one of my heroes.

When I met him, I could have just said, *"Uh, gee, it's nice to meet you. I'm a big fan."* But that would have been a missed opportunity.

Instead, I spent a few days thinking before I met him... I came up with a plan to make an impact – to give him a chance to want to get to know me...

I got out a 3x5 notecard. And I wrote out what I called "12 Ways to Take Over Your Industry." I included my name, phone number, and mail address. When I shook his hand, I smiled and I handed him the card. And that was that...

He could have easily thrown the card away. He could have thought, "*Who is this joker?*" He could have taken my suggestions... but still never bothered contacting me. For any number of reasons, he could have ignored me.

Instead, he reached out to me... In the end, he tried all of my dozen ideas, except one. Now, when he wants a second opinion on something (from outside of his corporate "yes" men), he sends me an e-mail or gives me a call. He has included me in events around the world and in his decisions that I've been grateful and flattered to be a part of.

The best part to me is that I can call a hero of mine a friend as well.

That didn't happen because I'm "lucky." It happened because of this simple secret. There are two parts to it...

1. Whenever there is any moment – any crack in the door to put your foot in to meet your hero – you must shove your foot in... and not let it out.

2. You must find a way to give a big benefit to your hero without asking anything in return.

Then you're off... At that point, you have done your best to kick off a potential legitimate friendship.

I have often had to create these moments. Usually, they don't just happen.

For example, I ended up on the phone with another hero of mine. He said: "*Next time you're in Nashville, give me a call and we can get together.*" Look, I'm NEVER in Nashville... but I went to Nashville that week. (I re-routed a flight to have a long layover there.)

I made it happen when the opportunity was there. And it was a fantastic few hours. Another hero of mine is now a friend of mine, too.

Most of the time, it doesn't work out this way. But it's 100% worth trying... Your downside risk is a little "wasted" effort. Your upside is a legitimate friendship with one of your heroes. That's worth it to me!

You can do it. You have to get creative to create the opportunity. You have to offer something that benefits your hero. And you have to do it without asking anything in return.

You have to create your "luck."

It has worked for me. I have been able to get close to many of my heroes – both in business and in my hobbies. And I believe it can work for you, too.

How cool is it to have your heroes as your friends? Just follow these tips, figure out your opportunity, and go for it... you can do it...

Chapter 11

I Just Figured Out the REAL Secret to My Success

Published July 18, 2013

I've finally figured out the REAL secret to my success. It's something I've unknowingly been doing my whole life.

I know I should have figured it out earlier. I'm in my 40s now... Just imagine where I'd be if I'd figured it out 20 years ago!

Unfortunately, many people never figure out the real secret to succeed. And I've never had a clear and simple way to explain it... until now.

One sentence from Venture Capitalist James Altucher's book, *Choose Yourself*, sums up the secret to my success: **The only way to create value for yourself is to create value for others**.

This is it... this is exactly what I've done.

I've always defined it differently in my own life. For example, in the previous chapter, I explained how I've become friends with my heroes.

What I do sounds simple... I offer huge "value" to them when given a chance. Importantly, I don't ask anything in return.

A good example is with another of my heroes, and now friend, Peter Churchouse.

Peter is one of the best investors in Asia. He recently started publishing his own investment research. And I wents out of my way to help him, without asking for anything in return. I flew Peter and his son to the U.S. so they could attend my publisher's private conference about improving our investment research business. I thought that it would be great for the best minds in the industry to meet Peter, and vice versa.

As Altucher wrote...

> Think of two people in your network who don't know each other but you think can add value to each other's lives.
>
> Introduce them... Get better and better at it. The more value that you bring to the people in your network (even if it doesn't bring value to you in an immediate way), the greater the value of your network. And then the greater value you will have.

So by connecting Peter to some of the best minds at Stansberry Research, I haven't just created value for him, I've created value for my "network," which has increased my own value.

But I think the most important part of this quote is: "...even if it doesn't bring value to you in an immediate way."

Over the years, I've trained many people, investing genuine effort in teaching them everything I know. There was no apparent benefit to me at the time. But now some of these people run my business for me way better than I ever could.

The rewards to me, both personally and financially, have been better than I could have ever imagined or hoped.

By investing genuine effort in someone, even without an apparent benefit, you start to build the "network" Altucher talks about.

And when things go well for the people you've sincerely helped, they remember you... They want to reward you with something – whether it's helping your business or giving you something else. Heck, sometimes the "something else" means even more...

A famous photographer (who I really respect) recently sent me a large photo of his from a gallery exhibition. He was thanking me for what I had done for him. I have never asked him for anything, he just chose to send it along with a note showing genuine passion and thankfulness. I hang it with pride in my home... Not only is it an awesome photo, I feel great about the reason it's on my wall.

For several years, I've been helping out one of the planet's best guitar builders, advising him about how to make good business decisions. I love his work, and I do it because I love it. I've never asked for anything in return, not even a discount on a guitar.

He's not a wealthy man, but as a gift, he gave me his first prototype guitar. This guitar has been played and signed by some of the best guitar players in the world. To me, you can't put a value on this guitar. It's an incredible instrument with an amazing story, and it's something incredibly important to my friend... something he felt I should have.

Remember what Altucher wrote: "The only way to create value for yourself is to create value for others."

I didn't realize it until I read *Choose Yourself*, but that is exactly what I do, and it has always created value for me – both financially and personally.

So the real secret to my success is that I've continually created value for others... which has dramatically increased my own value.

If you want to increase your own success, both financially and personally, start looking for ways to create value for others. I am living proof that your good deeds eventually come back around...

– Chapter 12 –

Seven Secrets From the Smartest Businessman I Know

Published September 9, 2009

My boss is the smartest guy I know...

I'm not just saying it because he signs my paychecks. Seriously, I mean it. He does things most bosses don't do. It has made him a wealthy man. And it has made many of his employees more money than they'd ever dreamed of.

I have a unique perspective here... I hired him 13 years ago. We've known each other since we were kids. Now, rightly, he's my boss.

He worked his way up from the bottom to the top. It wasn't because of some sort of power-mad ambition. He didn't have a master plan. He simply thought of better ways to do things.

What does he do that's different? What does he do that has made him more successful in a shorter period than anyone else?

He's not afraid to be proven wrong. I'm not saying he likes being wrong... He's a competitor. But he won't hold stupidly to his original belief once it has been discredited.

Ever since we were kids, he has had a unique ability to lead the troops in one direction, full speed ahead... Then if he's proven wrong, he'll do an immediate about-face and lead the charge in the opposite direction.

If a business idea isn't working, cut it. Don't waste valuable time trying to make a wrong a right. Surprisingly, most smart people have a hard time with this.

In a business deal, he does an outstanding job explaining what's in it for the other guy. In short, he doesn't talk about himself, his wants, and his needs... at all. He talks about the benefits for the guy on the other side of the table.

Like everyone, the guy on the other side of the table is selfish. When you get down to it, that guy doesn't care what's in it for you. But if you can convince him you'll make him more successful at what he does, you'll get your deal.

He praises and constructively criticizes people equally. If you're screwing up, my boss will call you out. So when the praise comes from him, everyone knows it's legitimate. It's valuable.

If you're the boss, you know constant praise without constructive criticism is useless. (Unfortunately, that's my management style. I'm too nice.)

He's friendly with "rivals." He even gives away most of our secrets. I didn't understand this one at first. I'm sure our competitors still don't...

Why would we happily give away our secrets? Well, after spending time with us, our competitors often end up wanting to partner. That grows their business, which grows ours... And if a rival's business folds, the employees know us and try to get a job. We end up with the best talent.

You might not like the idea of inviting your rivals over to share your secrets. But it makes great sense for both sides.

(My boss says, "I don't mind giving our secrets away... They'll never execute them like we can." That is the biggest insight of all.)

He hires people smarter than him. Wait, didn't I say he's the smartest guy I know? He's brilliant, yes. But he's not that organized. So when he decides to push our business into new areas, he hires the best guys he can find.

He pays his employees well – through pay incentives. He's done a fantastic job tying his employees' pay to the jobs he needs them to do.

In my own case, he's always structured my pay in a way that should 1) increase my income and 2) push me to put my efforts behind the best opportunity he sees.

Lastly and most importantly... it's not about the money. The money is simply one "scoreboard" of his success. A lot of it is about fun... about coming up with a business idea and seeing if it works.

If you took all his money away tomorrow and told him he had to move to a different country, pick a place where he didn't speak the language, and find a different industry, he'd make all that money back again in the same short amount of time. He'd use all his secrets... like the handful I outlined above... and he'd do it. No question about it.

Some of these secrets might sound backward at first. But if one sounds "totally wrongheaded," think long and hard about it... My boss is the smartest guy I know... and I've seen him do these things over and over again.

You should try to do the same.

THE WISE INVESTOR

– Chapter 13 –

It's Time to Change Your Thinking About Making Money

February 8, 2017

I invest in a simple way...

I'm willing to concede a few battles to win the war.

This is a simple idea. Unfortunately, most investors can't do it. It goes against our egos to simply admit that we might be wrong and move on. We think we need to be right EVERY SINGLE time.

What's the war we're trying to win? Growing our net worth.

And to grow your net worth, you have to start by knowing that you are NOT going to win every time in investing. It's not going to happen...

You are going to win some, and you are going to lose some. Let me repeat that last part: **You are going to lose some**.

You need to be OK with this.

Knowing that you are going to lose some, you have a simple mission: **You must take steps to make sure your winners are larger than your losers**.

This is where nearly all investors fail. But that doesn't have to be you...

I turn it into a simple math problem... I make sure my losers stay small by cutting them early. And I let my winners grow.

It's the old saying... "Cut your losers and let your winners ride."

Let's take a quick look at some easy math so you can see how important this is...

Let's say you made three consecutive trades. By the time you closed out, the returns were: -10%, -10%, and +100%.

How did you do?

You might think that you did poorly... Your median return was -10%. That sounds terrible – no question.

Also, you were wrong 67% of the time. That sounds bad, right? Who wants to lose money on two out of three trades?

But I would take these three trades any day...

Here's what really happened: In this scenario, $100,000 invested would have turned into $162,000.

You would have made a 62% return on these three trades. And that holds true regardless of the order you placed them in...

$100,000 would have turned into $90,000 after the first losing trade, and then $81,000 after the second losing trade. Then it would have doubled to $162,000 after the winning trade.

Flipping the order around gives the same result: $100,000 would have turned into $200,000 on the first trade... Then it would have fallen to $180,000, and finished at $162,000.

How does turning $100,000 into $162,000 in three trades sound to you? It sounds pretty good to me!

All it takes is cutting your losers early and letting your winners ride.

You make sure your losses stayed small... And you let your winner ride.

So how do you trade? Do you cut your losers early and let your winners ride?

If not, then it's time for a change... You need to realize that it's OK to lose some battles on the way to winning the war.

Here's the thing... You will not be right every time. I promise. What matters is what you do when you are wrong.

What is your plan? Most people don't have one. And that will crush them, eventually.

If you don't have a plan, I suggest changing your thinking about making money. Set yourself up for sustained success. Start cutting those losers early... and letting those winners ride.

Chapter 14

What's the Point of Investing?

Published April 11, 2008

"Nice to meet you... Hang on a sec... Let me text my husband."

My wife and I stand there waiting. The young woman busily taps out a text message on her new iPhone.

She's not so quick with the typing, but we know what's going on... She's just showing off that she owns a $500 phone – hot stuff in rural Georgia.

We saw her arrive... She drove a black Suburban of some sort, with enough chrome to make a Detroit drug dealer blush.

She and her husband are young... probably in their late 20s. He's apparently a builder in Georgia. Of course, homebuilding in Georgia died about two years ago... But even though their income must be down, their spending hasn't changed.

This young woman isn't the only one out here sporting an iPhone and a blingy black Suburban. What's going on here?

Me? I don't have an iPhone or a blingy Suburban... But I probably have one thing these conspicuous consumers don't: The house I live in is fully paid for.

I handle my money differently. I *could* buy an iPhone or a Suburban tomorrow. I wouldn't need a penny of debt to do it. But I won't... Why?

Because I know those things won't make me the slightest bit happier. I'd be the same dolt I was before... only now, I'd be $50,000 poorer!

It took me a while to get to this point in my life. But I'm glad I made it... I'm at the point where I can buy what I want. But I don't. It's an important point to reach.

I don't try to keep up with the Joneses. I'm doing the opposite, actually. I'm downsizing. I'm reducing my "stuff."

Think about this... What good is all this stuff, really? You can't take it with you when you die... Again, legendary newsletter writer Doug Casey says it best: *"I've never seen a hearse with luggage racks."*

Doug is extremely wealthy and has been for a while. But when he joined us in Georgia, he didn't arrive in a blingy Suburban and he wasn't chatting on an iPhone.

My friend Bob Bishop is a wealthy guy like Doug. Bob wrote the excellent *Gold Mining Stock Report* newsletter for a few decades. When he retired, Bob decided to sell some of his extraordinary possessions... for no reason I could see. He didn't need the money. And they weren't taking up space. I asked him why he was selling. He said...

> After a while, you don't own your stuff... Your stuff owns you. Steve, you're young... so you're probably in the accumulation phase. Me? I've been there. Now I want to downsize and simplify. I don't need all this stuff.

Bob can buy anything he wants. But like Doug, he doesn't drive a blingy Suburban, and I doubt he's got an iPhone. It's just stuff!

What's the point of saving money anyway? What's the point of investing?

When you get older (if you're not already older!), just what are you going to buy with that money you've saved?

Jonathan Clements gave a good answer to this in his farewell column for the *Wall Street Journal*. (Clements has written more than 1,000 columns for the *Wall Street Journal*.)

Clements says your savings *"can deliver three key benefits."*

Even better, he says, *"You can enjoy this trio of benefits even if you don't have great wads of cash."* **These key benefits are the main point of investing**...

1. If you have money, you don't have to worry about it.

2. Money can give you the freedom to pursue your passions.

3. Money can buy you time with friends and family.

These three things are exactly what Doug and Bob are doing with their lives. The great thing is, it doesn't (usually) take millions to spend time with friends and family or pursue your passions. **You don't need a fortune to live well**.

But to get there, the Georgia homebuilder couple needs to skip out on his and hers blingmobiles.

The quicker you grasp this about saving versus spending, the quicker you'll be able to start living like Doug and Bob... even if you don't have many millions in the bank.

You might think it's hard to stop buying ultimately useless stuff... You might think it's hard to stop keeping up with the Joneses.

But actually, it's liberating... And even better, you'll be financially free much quicker. So give it a try.

– Chapter 15 –

The Right Person to Look After Your Money

Published July 15, 2013

This is one of life's biggest questions...

Answer this question correctly, and you could live a life of peace and happiness as your wealth steadily grows.

Answer this question incorrectly, and you could end up broke, like the victims you see every night on CNBC's *American Greed*.

You really don't want to get this question wrong. Here it is...

Who is the right person to look after your money?

My dad made a surprising decision on this topic decades ago...

He didn't make many bad decisions in his incredible life. But I questioned one decision he made when I'd just graduated from college...

You see, right after college, I became a stockbroker... And after a few months on the job, my dad transferred a good portion of his financial net worth over to me to look after.

I didn't understand my dad's decision...

I was flattered that he trusted me like this... But I was overwhelmed.

I didn't want to do anything wrong. Also, I knew there were more experienced people at my firm who could do a better job for him. So why me?

I didn't get it decades ago... but I get it today...

The right person to look out for your money is YOU.

The longer it takes for you to figure this out, the more money you will lose.

Nobody cares more about your money than you do. And nobody will look after it better than you will.

When I say that YOU are the right person to look out for your money, I don't mean that you have to do all the research and trading. You can work with brokers and insurance agents. You need to rely on experts, of course. What I mean is this...

You can't give up knowing what's going on with your money.

My dad didn't just turn over his money to me blindly. He was very active with me. It was fun. We discussed every decision... every trade. We talked about the markets regularly. We talked about everything we did before we did it.

That's the way to do it... you don't just do things blindly because someone says so. That's how you end up getting hurt.

You see it every day... In the news, you hear about pro athletes and rap stars going broke because they weren't looking out for their own money. It's their fault – they made a choice to not be responsible. They made a choice to pay someone to handle their money for them. And too many times, giving up responsibility cost them everything they have.

Instead, you should do your research and talk about this stuff. Don't just throw your hands up and give up responsibility.

My dad didn't give up his responsibility. He knew what was going on with his money. He made good decisions about his advisors. And he stayed on top of what they were doing.

(We really learned this when he died suddenly. He had his act together, with excellent records and paperwork... That's something I need to do a better job of for my family.)

Not all of his money decisions were great, of course. He had a bit of a speculative streak, and my mom would give him a hard time about the ones that didn't work out. (He deserved it!) But that's fine... because in the long run, **my dad made the only "right" decision that he really needed to make with his money**.

He knew that the only right person to look after his money was him. And he knew that didn't mean he had to do everything himself...

What it means is, you can't ever give up knowing what's going on with your money. Nobody will look out for your money better than YOU. Don't forget that...

Chapter 16

The Biggest Lie:
'It Takes Money to Make Money'

Published November 5, 2012

"Congrats Steve, you just made $100,000 today," a lawyer said to me this week.

I just bought a property... cheap. The lawyer thinks I could sell it for a six-figure profit right away.

A friend of mine heard about this deal and said, *"Well... it takes money to make money."*

I was surprised he said that... To me, this little phrase is one of the biggest and most dangerous lies out there... It is a convenient excuse to simply not try to succeed.

It's like the old joke:

> *"Lord, I've worked hard all my life, why couldn't you have just let me win the lottery?"*
>
> The Lord replied, *"Why didn't you just buy a ticket?"*

You've got to try. And it doesn't "take money to make money"... In my last real estate deal, one of my business partners put up no money at all... Instead, he put in "sweat equity."

He did most of the work on this project, adding value to our investment. I'm certain he will come out with a six-figure profit when we sell. He could even make a *couple hundred thousand dollars*!

Remember, he put zero money in. So in his case, it didn't "take money to make money."

His situation is not unique in real estate... A common deal goes like this... A young guy comes up with an idea to make money. He finds a property he can buy for $100,000, put $20,000 into, and sell for $150,000.

The problem is, he has no money. So he finds an old guy with money, and they agree to split the profits 50/50. If the deal goes according to plan, they both walk away with a $15,000 profit.

He had the only two things you need: 1) an idea and 2) the willingness to roll up his sleeves and make it happen... He did everything from finding the old guy and convincing him to invest, all the way through to selling the property.

In both examples, the young guy didn't even have any risk in the deal. Real estate deals are an easy example. But it doesn't "take money to make money" in other areas, either...

A young friend of mine came up with a simple idea. He launched a website that focuses on – get this – forklifts! It's like a Hotels.com, only for heavy-duty equipment. If you need to buy or rent heavy equipment, you can locate... through his website... the pieces you need that are closest to you and at the best prices.

It's not the sexiest-sounding business... But it's a great idea. It cost him next to nothing to set his website up and call equipment owners to get them onboard.

Now he earns a commission from every sale or rental. Life is good. He doesn't work for "the man" anymore and hasn't for years. And he's making more money than ever.

It doesn't take money to make money. You just need two things…

1. A great idea

2. To roll up your sleeves and make it happen

You can't underestimate either of those things. The amount of effort and commitment required will be extraordinary. But that's the way it goes. You're trying to break out of the ordinary. So an ordinary effort won't cut it. You will need to sustain an extraordinary effort.

This is hard. But it's how you make money.

It is much easier to give up. It is much easier to say, "It takes money to make money" and never try. It is much easier to complain that you'll never win the lottery and never buy a ticket. (You know what I mean.)

Don't ever catch yourself saying it takes money to make money.

It doesn't… It takes a great idea and the willingness to make it happen. Now get to it! You can do it.

Chapter 17

Exactly What I Do With My Own Money

March 1, 2016

"How do you invest your own money, Steve?"

People ask me that all the time...

Some of these folks are looking for a very technical answer (like what percentages I invest in stocks and bonds, and how I come up with those).

Others are actually just looking for a hot tip. (The best hot tip is this: There is no such thing as a hot tip!)

I will share with you what I do with my own money today...

Upfront, you need to know that what I do with my money is probably NOT the right thing for you to do with your money.

I break "the rules"...

However, if you know the rules, and if you are strong enough to cut your losses when necessary, you can consider doing what I do...

I can sum up what I do with my own money very simply:

I wait for the fat pitch.

I am often "under-invested." I don't typically own a lot of stocks just because "I'm supposed to." Instead, I wait for an extraordinary situation – a fat pitch.

The idea of "the fat pitch" comes from the most successful investor of all time... Warren Buffett. He said:

> I call investing the greatest business in the world because you never have to swing. You stand at the plate, the pitcher throws you General Motors at 47! U.S. Steel at 39! and nobody calls a strike on you. There's no penalty except opportunity lost. All day you wait for the pitch you like; then when the fielders are asleep, you step up and hit it.

Fat pitches don't happen often. Sometimes you have to wait years for them to appear.

For example, I thought my fat-pitch opportunity in U.S. real estate would never appear...

I'd been an investor for decades, but I'd never bought U.S. real estate as an investment.

It was never cheap enough for my standards. It was never a fat pitch.

I thought I'd gotten it wrong. Plenty of people around me had gotten rich through real estate. But I had an aversion to borrowing money... And I didn't see the dramatic upside potential.

Then it happened... We had the worst real estate bust in generations. And mortgage rates hit their lowest levels in generations. I got my fat pitch. And I swung, starting in 2011.

Before the "great bust" in the U.S. real estate market, I had never bought any property in the U.S. (except for my home) – because I never saw my fat pitch. Now, Florida real estate is the biggest part of my investment portfolio, by far.

Fat pitches like the great real estate bust don't come along every day. Personally, I have been very patient...

I swung the bat just three times in the last 10 years.

Here's what I did:

Fat Pitch No. 1: In late 2008, I saw a fat pitch coming in stocks. I bought all I could – and I even took out a home-equity loan to buy even more. That's the only time I've ever done that. I was a bit early – the real bottom was March 2009. But it worked out fantastically... I paid off the home-equity loan a little more than a year later out of my profits.

Fat Pitch No. 2: In 2011, I started buying Florida real estate heavily. I may have gone overboard... but the fat pitch was too good. In one deal, I bought a couple hundred acres *for 90% less* than they were worth under contract just two years before. And just last week, I signed a contract to sell a condo for twice what I paid for it – less than three and a half years ago.

Fat Pitch No. 3: In late 2015, I started building up a portfolio of microcap gold-mining stocks. This sector had lost more than 90% of its value in the previous four years. It was the cheapest it had been in a generation, at least.

Like U.S. real estate a few years ago, I had never invested a significant chunk of my money in gold stocks before.

By buying small gold stocks in late 2015, I was a full three months early... Fortunately, I didn't lose much. Importantly, I cut my losers when they hit new lows, and I added to my winners. Then... gold stocks soared!

Waiting on "the fat pitch" works for me...

It is challenging.

I think about life in a unique way... I think that 98% of the time, life is ordinary. The other 2% of life is extraordinary moments...

If you are capable of recognizing those "2% moments" and acting on them to the fullest extent possible, then you can potentially generate extraordinary returns.

I am constantly on the lookout for those extraordinary moments in life and in investing, and I try to make the most of them.

Whether this way of thinking is right or not doesn't actually matter... I believe it – and it works for me!

Again, I am not suggesting that you follow my "fat-pitch" way of investing. But if you want to know what I do with my own money, and how I think about it... now you know.

Chapter 18

What You NEED to Know to Be a Successful Investor

Published August 28, 2012

"Steve, I'm just trying to get all this stuff figured out," my friend Charlie told me. He had just starting out in investing.

"I'm paralyzed," he said. *"I don't know what to do. I'm reading everything... But I'm not actually doing anything with my money."*

"Charlie, you're doing the right thing," I said. *"Learning first – and not doing anything stupid with your money – is exactly the right thing to do."*

Charlie is not alone...

You or someone you know may be in a similar situation. So let's look at some of the important basics of successful investing.

These are helpful for beginning and seasoned investors... They're a great reminder about the most important things to understand when it comes to the market.

1. You aren't going to get rich overnight through investing.

A proper investment is one that has at least a two-year horizon. Said another way... Any investment that can double your money in a month is likely risky. You could lose all your money just as quickly. If you don't adjust your thinking in line with this, chances are you'll end up losing a lot of money.

2. Start small. That keeps your investing "tuition cost" low.

I don't mean "tuition cost" in the traditional sense... I call your
"investing tuition" the money that you inevitably lose on your first
investments because of something you didn't know or understand.
Start small, and keep that tuition cost low.

3. Don't invest in something you don't understand.

One of the fastest ways to lose money is to put your funds into
something you don't really understand. If you don't understand how
you'll make money on the investment – and you can't point out your
risks – you are not ready for that investment. Go study some more. And
if you still don't understand, simply skip that investment.

4. What's a good return in a low-interest-rate environment?

Is 5% a good return? In the early 2000s, 5% was a bad return... But
when banks are paying near-0% interest, 5% is (sadly) a good return on
your safe money.

5. Where should you invest now?

Younger investors (under age 50) should focus their learning on
property and the stock market. Both property (in Florida, at least) and
stocks are the best values they've been in decades (with the exception
of the March 2009 bottom in stocks). I could be wrong. You could lose
money. But I think these are your best shots at making "real" money
investing.

6. Don't put all your eggs in one basket.

Don't put your entire net worth in one property... And make sure you
spread your stock holdings around as well by first investing in funds
that hold a bunch of stocks. Something like the SPDR Dow Jones
Industrial Average Fund (DIA) – which holds 30 stocks, including
IBM, ExxonMobil, and Wal-Mart – is a good, "one click" way to own a
basket of stocks.

7. History repeats – or at least it rhymes.

It's amazing how investors never learn that history repeats. The recent bust in property prices is a good example. In 2006, people thought property prices could never go down. Then, people thought property prices could never go up again. The truth is somewhere in between.

Keep in mind… you want to SELL an investment when it's expensive and everybody loves it (like housing in 2006). And you want to BUY an investment when everybody hates it (like housing today). But…

8. Don't fight the trend.

To increase your odds of making money, you don't want to try to catch a falling knife. That is gambling, not investing. Instead, it is much safer to grab that knife once it has hit and settled a bit. In other words, don't buy a stock that is going down. Instead, buy something that has started going up…

9. Cut your losses early.

There's no better way to prevent massive losses than to set – and stick to – an exit strategy on every investment you make. It's the simplest thing you can do to continually increase the value of your portfolio. The best way to do this is a "trailing stop" (as we discussed in Part One, Chapter 8).

10. When in doubt, don't do it.

If you have any doubt about putting your money into a new investment… don't do it. Instead, keep reading and learning. That keeps your investing "tuition cost" way down!

These are rules to live by. And they're not just for beginners. Every investor – experienced or novice – should stick to these rules.

As for my friend Charlie… by reading and researching first – and not putting money to work yet – he made all the right moves.

I urge you to follow Charlie's lead. Learn as much as you can about the markets and investing. Follow these 10 rules. And you should be successful.

– Chapter 19 –

How I Know When I'm Wrong, and How I Get Out

October 11, 2016

What happens if things go wrong? When do I "get out"?

Let me turn the question back on you... When do YOU get out? At what point do you KNOW you're wrong?

What? You don't know?

This is YOUR MONEY. You worked hard for it. And you're just "winging it"? You're just "shooting from the hip"? Really?

We've got to change that, RIGHT NOW...

I have a perfect example of how I know I'm wrong in a trade... and when it's time to get out.

The example is real. My paid subscribers just went through it last week. I will tell you what the investment is – but frankly, *that doesn't matter*. What matters is the lesson.

Less than a month ago, I recommended that my subscribers buy the British pound...

The British pound had fallen to its lowest level in 30 years. And it was extremely hated – speculators had placed large bets against it. But we saw the start of an uptrend in place. It was worth a speculation. So here's what I told my subscribers...

> By setting a stop loss at the recent low, we're only risking 2.3%. But if we're right, and the pound recovers from its valuation and sentiment extremes, we could easily see double-digit gains... We have a risk-to-reward ratio of roughly 4-to-1. And that's too good to pass up.

This is how I trade. It's all about the odds...

When you have the setup you want to see... and your upside potential is four times your downside risk, you enter the trade.

So we entered the trade. But we got stopped out for a 4% loss. No big deal. Then the big deal arrived... The bottom fell out of the British pound. Take a look...

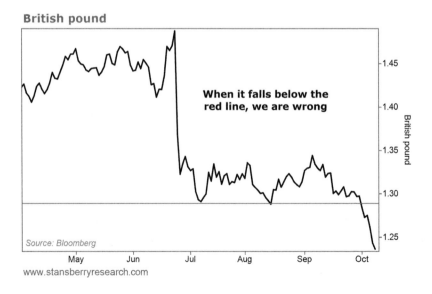

British pound

Source: Bloomberg

www.stansberryresearch.com

You can see the British pound had hit new lows in July and August. When we entered the trade in September, I said to GET OUT if the British pound closed below those lows because that would mean I was wrong.

The British pound closed below those lows. It was time to get out. People who followed my advice lost no more than 4%.

After that, the bottom fell out... And the British pound kept falling, and falling, and falling.

So let me ask you again... If you are "just winging it" or "shooting from the hip," when will you get out of a trend like this one? Now? Or will you buy more and double down?

What's your plan? Do you know your upside potential and your downside risk? You don't know if you don't have a plan.

I know when the market is telling me I am wrong about an investment idea (when it hits a new low).

Remember, I wait to buy until there's an uptrend in place. So a new closing low means that I am totally wrong about that uptrend. I get out the next day.

When are you wrong? When do you sell?

It's fine if your exit plan is different. (Trailing stop losses are a preferred method.) But my goodness, have a plan – and follow it!

– Chapter 20 –

What I Personally Use to Track My Investments

April 21, 2014

"How do you track your investments?"

"You tell us to use 'trailing stops'... but how do you track them?"

I get asked these questions all of the time.

Two truths...

1. We pay five figures a year in data and software, but...

2. You can do most of what we do for very little money.

We pay over $100,000 each year simply for data. (We typically get data from Bloomberg, Thomson Reuters Datastream, and more.)

However, you don't have to do this...

Most of the time, we don't use our expensive toys... because there are quicker ways to get what we need, with simpler tools. Even better, most of these simple tools are either free, or very inexpensive.

Let me show you...

To track our Trailing Stops every day, we use TradeStops.com. It sends out e-mail alerts when our trailing stops are hit. There's a free Trailing

Stops Calculator on the site, and you can try the TradeStops service free for a month. We liked TradeStops.com so much, our publisher invested in it. We use it every day.

We use Microsoft Excel for a lot of things. And we have a couple (free and inexpensive) add-ons that we really like...

We use XLQ software to track portfolios on Excel. XLQ brings all kinds of stock data into Excel. It's not just price data – it has fundamental data, trailing-stop data, and more. It's extraordinary. If you are an Excel user, you must check it out. You can try it for free for 45 days, and it's very reasonably priced beyond that.

For a quick check of financial news, we go to www.Bloomberg.com. For very quick looks at stocks, we still use Yahoo Finance (just because we're used to it).

When we need data beyond stock data, a great source that we rely on is the St. Louis Federal Reserve. The St. Louis Fed's website is incredibly easy to use – and it's free! Even better, if you're an Excel user, the St. Louis Fed has a fantastic free Excel Add-in that brings its data and charting capabilities directly into your Excel sheet.

All these things are self-updating, as well... When you open your Excel sheet, they update themselves with the latest data.

We do pay BIG MONEY for a mountain of data.

But we could do most of our research with what I've shared with you here... and most of it is either free or very inexpensive.

These are truly the actual tools we use every day.

If you were curious about what we rely on – what we use to track the markets and our stocks, and to do our jobs well – then the secret is out. Now you know.

– Chapter 21 –

The Nearly Infallible Cocktail-Party Indicator

Published January 18, 2008

"What's wrong with Steve?" I bet people have said about me many times.

"Why is he always talking about some ridiculous sounding investment?"

That's the cocktail-party crowd... I just can't win.

But cocktail parties are where I learn where NOT to invest. They're the perfect "contrary" indicator. You can, and should, use the cocktail-party indicator to save your investments.

In short, **you can take whatever investment idea EVERYONE is talking about, and you can just about guarantee that it'll be substantially lower within five years**. The thing is, when everyone is talking about an investment idea, you can be sure it's just about run its course. It's time to think about moving on...

For example, in 2005, all the talk at the cocktail parties was real estate. *"You can't go wrong in real estate,"* everyone agreed. *"Real estate has never had a down year."*

Usually, I'd keep my thoughts to myself. Sometimes I might say, *"What about Japan? Just like the States, it barely had a down year from 1950 to 1990 – then it fell for 17 straight years."* But people would look at me like I was from Mars. I shouldn't have opened my mouth.

It gets worse... Some folks would then ask me, "*So what are you buying?*"

"*Oh, I'm buying gold,*" I'd say. The look I usually got was an involuntary wince of pain. No words were needed.

If they had listened, they would have made triple-digit returns. After doing this for a long time, **I've learned *the stronger the wince, the greater your potential returns***.

The thing is, the cocktail-party cycle repeats... over and over again. It becomes – dare I say it – easy. You can almost learn what to buy... and definitely what to sell, simply from paying attention to the cocktail-party crowd.

As one more example, back in 1998-1999, young people were going after the dot-com jobs. And older folks were buying shares of anything with "com" in it. It was the "new economy," and everyone was entitled to get rich. But in the January 2000 Annual Forecast issue of the Oxford Club newsletter, I told readers in no uncertain terms: "*We are at the peak of most likely the greatest financial mania that will ever be seen in our lifetimes and quite possibly the greatest ever witnessed.*"

So when I started my *True Wealth* newsletter in 2001, we went the exact opposite of dot-coms... In the very first issue, we started buying real estate. Everything in real estate was cheap. It was completely ignored. And yet the uptrend had begun. So we bought stocks that owned commercial real estate, apartments, shopping centers, you name it.

Once again, I don't think many people took us up on our advice. They wanted "tech" not "stuff." They wanted what had already gone up over the last few years. But "tech" was expensive. "Stuff" was cheap. And subscribers who took my advice made triple-digit profits on several real estate stocks.

Back then, commodities also seemed easy to me. We need commodities – agriculture, metals, oil, etc. Yet commodity producers hadn't increased their capacity in more than 20 years.

We had a simple situation... Demand was growing exponentially. And with no new mines in 20 years, supply couldn't grow. Yet prices were low. It was Economics 101, prices were about to go nuts.

"Commodities always go down in price," I was told. *"You never make money in commodities."* This time, it wasn't just the cocktail-party crowd that told me how ridiculous that idea was. Academics told me I was ridiculous. And so did money managers.

Yet when people tell me *"you never make money in commodities,"* I see it in a different way... It tells me that nobody is looking at them – and that there might be all kinds of opportunities that haven't been looked at yet. I start to think about buying them.

My *True Wealth* readers made great returns in various commodity-related investments in the following years. But in 2008, commodities were finally becoming legitimate.

I heard one investment advisor on CNBC say, *"You've got to have 20% of your assets in commodities. Me, personally, I have 40% of my assets in commodities."*

Oh no! We were coming full circle. Commodity prices went on to crash soon after.

The cocktail-party indicator is the first nearly infallible warning sign that a big trend is nearing an end. It's accurate, and you don't need any particular skills (other than willpower) to follow it.

Remember this indicator. It'll save you a fortune by keeping you from following the crowd.

Chapter 22

Gotta Jump On It! Or You'll Miss It

Published April 4, 2011

"You got a great deal on that investment," my friend Geoff Anandappa told me over breakfast. "We definitely don't offer terms like that anymore."

In 2006, I bought a "guaranteed investment contract" from Geoff through his firm, Stanley Gibbons, in London.

When I first learned about it, the deal seemed too good to be true. So I did as much "homework" on the idea as I could. Then I flew to London to be certain. It checked out. It was legitimate.

The terms were too good... **My worst-case outcome was a positive 7% annual return, for 10 years**. My best case was dramatically higher returns... and my potential for profits was unlimited.

My risk was the company itself – would Stanley Gibbons be around in 10 years to pay me? The answer was yes... Stanley Gibbons has been around more than 150 years. Since it traded on the stock market, its financial information was public knowledge, and I learned the company had no debt. This was an incredible opportunity.

Once I did my homework and believed it was legitimate, I leaped! I became the first person to buy the 10-year contracts.

These days, Stanley Gibbons no longer offers guaranteed investment contracts like that. If I hadn't jumped on it, I couldn't have done it, ever. The same type of thing happened to me with tax-lien certificates...

If I hadn't jumped, I would have missed it.

You see, in 2009, I could buy all the tax-lien certificates I wanted in my county in Florida at 18% interest. So in 2010, I was all set to do it again... But tax-lien bidding was so competitive, I didn't buy a single one. If I hadn't taken advantage of the original 18% opportunity, I would have missed it.

These are just two examples of what I'm talking about.

When you come across an investment opportunity that seems too good to be true, you have two possible outcomes...

1. It's not true. You're either missing something in the fine print or it's a scam.

2. It's legitimate.

Frankly, 99% of the time, it IS too good to be true. So you must check it out diligently. If anything – I mean anything – smells wrong or shady about the deal, it probably is. Do as much homework as you possibly can. Talk to people you trust, and listen without emotion (as best as you can) to the red flags they raise.

Then trust your instincts. **Don't let your greed cloud the facts**.

The 1% of great deals that are legitimate just about always fall in one of two categories...

Either they're completely ignored (like the Stanley Gibbons deal or tax-lien certificates)... or they're completely hated (like real estate, where you might find a "too good to be true" deal).

Too-good-to-be-true investment opportunities do exist... 99% of the time, they're not what they seem. For the other 1%, they disappear as soon as the rest of the world figures them out.

When you find one of these, **check it out thoroughly... and then jump**. Don't hesitate.

For me, I'm typically too cautious. In the past, I'd discover great ideas but not jump when I needed to. So I'd miss 'em.

Now, I jump. Whether it's a stock market bottom or a little-known idea like I described above, I don't hesitate anymore. I jump.

If you're already prone to leaping before looking, you probably don't need my encouragement here. But if you're like most people, you want to wait for... well, I don't know what... but you want to wait.

Don't wait. First, do your homework. And if it checks out, leap!

I've made the biggest profits in my investments by doing exactly that.

– Chapter 23 –

Is That a Legitimate Shot at a 200% Gain? Or Just a Headache?

Published January 5, 2012

"Steve, you've got to think of every one of these deals as buying another headache... Do you really want THIS PARTICULAR headache?"

My friend Brad Thomason gave me that advice a few years ago, and it stuck.

I'd asked him for his advice... I was interested in a tiny property investment deal that I thought was a "slam dunk." I called Brad for his advice because he sizes up thousands of potential property deals similar to this one each year.

Based on Brad's advice, I didn't do the deal. And I'm sure glad I didn't...

If I'd done the deal, I would have been taking on a big headache that, in the long run, wouldn't have been worth it...

While the return percentage would have been high, the actual dollar return wouldn't have been that high – particularly considering the amount of time and effort I would have needed to put in.

And that's the crucial point.

I've repeated Brad's advice to myself (*"Do you really want THIS PARTICULAR headache?"*) many times since then... and I've kept myself headache-free.

151

Brad and I met up yesterday on the courthouse steps of a county auctioning off distressed real estate.

Dozens of properties sold... But we didn't bite on anything. The best property sold had a tax-assessed value of $266,000 – and it ended up selling for $40,000.

Buying a $266,000 property for $40,000 sounds like a good deal to me. It seems like you could have potentially made a 200% return on that property.

Brad didn't bid on it. And he didn't lose any sleep over it. In his case, he didn't need THIS PARTICULAR headache. That deal would have been a small one for his business. It was nowhere near his office or any of his other operations. So he decided he didn't need to spin his wheels on it.

I thought it showed restraint and judgment on Brad's part... He could have made a big percentage return on his investment. But for his actual business, it wouldn't have been that big a dollar return, relative to the time and effort required. So he passed.

The best investors and businessmen I know fully understand this idea, and they implement it every day. They know which particular headaches are worth taking on.

I remember a publisher in my industry telling me (more than once), "Steve, that's a good idea... But since it won't make $500,000, we can't spend our time on it."

He wasn't being arrogant or condescending... He is simply a keen businessman. He understands the value of his time and the value of his employees' time. This publisher had the restraint and judgment to know it was better to either improve my idea or find a bigger one, than waste time on a smaller idea.

I also worked for a billion-dollar New York hedge-fund manager, and he understood this concept. My marching orders were simple: Find any investment idea that can potentially make a profit of $25 million or more.

Easier said than done! But by having this mandate, the fund manager didn't end up with 1,000 little investment ideas to watch. Instead, he ended up with a couple dozen ideas that he got to know REALLY well.

The point is, just because an investment could make you a big return, *doesn't mean you should do it.*

Remember that each business deal or investment you enter into is another "headache." It will require effort to monitor and move forward. You have to ask yourself if this is the particular headache you want.

Brad passed on the $40,000 deal. That kept his head and his time clear for a larger property deal closer to his home that he's excited about, one that could net his fund $1 million-plus in profits over a couple years. I saw the publisher I wrote about pass on certain profits as well.

They both were smart to do it...

The best investors and businessmen I know have a remarkable ability to say "no" to many likely profitable ideas, simply because they're not worth the headache.

Once you take on this mindset, you'll find actual deals that are worth your time and hassle are rare. You'll learn to take on projects only when they're worth it... And you'll have the energy to make those deals count.

Chapter 24

Get Rich Investing...
No Special Skills Required

Published January 6, 2011

Want to get rich investing?

I'll show you how I've succeeded... The great thing about what I do is you can do it, too. No special skills are required.

You don't need to be a math or computer whiz. You don't need to spend all your waking hours watching stock quotes on your computer or CNBC.

All you need is patience, guts, some money to start, and two rules...

I've spent my career studying the financial markets starting in the early 1990s... crunching the numbers in every possible way. I've gone as far as possible with my education. I've run research departments, managed funds, and traveled the world looking at investment ideas.

But now that I've done all that, I can tell you that *you don't need all that stuff*.

You just need to know two simple things...

1. You want to buy when everyone is terrified, but things aren't as bad as they think. To reduce your risk even more, you want to wait for the uptrend.

2. You want to sell (or at least get ready to sell) when everyone is optimistic.

That's it. Extremely simple. No complicated math required. Of course, I crunch numbers to help me pinpoint exactly when we're seeing these things. But you don't NEED to.

It's obvious when everyone is terrified or when everyone is optimistic and feeling greedy... You don't need a computer to tell you. And you can see a clear uptrend on a chart with your eyeballs – no number-crunching required.

In March 2009, we had the perfect buy setup. Everyone was terrified. But things couldn't possibly have been as bad as everyone thought.

The stock market bottomed on March 9, 2009. And on March 20, after seeing the start of an uptrend, I said to buy. The headline of my March 20 essay was "A Dramatic Turn for the Better, Time to Buy Stocks."

The opportunity was as good as it gets. For the only time in my life, I personally borrowed money (through a home equity line) to buy stocks.

Stocks are up 93% since bottoming on March 9, as measured by the total return on the S&P 500 Index. [***Editor's note****: As of mid-2017, stocks are up about 220% since bottoming in 2009.*] If you took on a little more risk (as I did, buying things like an India hedge fund), you did much better.

I've made my biggest gains when investors are terrified and things are stealthily getting less bad. That's the recipe for big gains. Trade accordingly.

– Chapter 25 –

The Courage to Get Rich

Published March 1, 2006

Rick Rule lives well...

He spends the winter in New Zealand (because it's summer there). He spends the summer in Vancouver, Canada. And in fall and spring, he's in southern California.

In New Zealand, Rick has more than 1,000 acres, on the ocean. I visited him there. While my kids played on the beach, Rick told me...

"Steve, I've got to thank you... a few years ago, you told me something that's really made me a lot of money."

Rick is one of the smartest guys I've ever met. After 30-plus years in the investment business, most of it spent running his own brokerage/ investment banking firm, he knows money.

Rick has a lot more experience than me. But we're both in the same game... figuring out how to turn money into more money. The game is hard, but it's a lot of fun to both of us.

"So what was it that I told you, Rick?" I asked him.

"I remember it plain as day... It was at an Investment U conference. You told me, 'Rick, you've got to have the courage to be right.'"

Maybe he remembered that because it's not very often successful money men like Rick get told how to do things. (It's even rarer if they actually take the advice.)

Rick went on...

> Steve, you were right.
>
> For decades, I've bought things at 50 cents on the dollar, and I've sold when those things approached fair value. You told me that I was leaving a mountain of the gains on the table... that you never know how high something could go... and that you can simply use a mental trailing stop to both protect yourself and, more importantly, to potentially get out at a much higher price.
>
> **You told me to have the courage to be right**.

To me, if Rick is doing this now, he's the complete investor. He's got it all...

Better than almost anyone, Rick knows how to buy valuable assets cheaply. Now, he's using a technique to maximize the value of his hard work. He has the courage to not only make good money, but to make even more on his ideas.

At this point, I don't think Rick needs much more money. I think he just loves the game, like I do. It just happens the scorecards in this game are the account values... both his and his clients'.

The game is simple. As they always say... you buy low and sell high.

The technique we can use to sell high is a simple idea called a trailing stop.

As a rough rule, I recommend using a 25% trailing stop in my newsletter *True Wealth*. So if we own a stock at $10, it goes to $20, and then it falls by 25% to $15 a share, I get out. It's down 25% from its high since I bought it – but I'm guaranteed to lock in a 50% gain from my entry price.

As an example... back in 1999, my boss Porter Stansberry recommended buying shares of JDS Uniphase (JDSU) in the newsletter I was heading at the time, *The Oxford Club*. The stock soared more than 1,000% before falling by 25%. We sold when this happened, pocketing around 900% gains. The stock kept falling, right back down to where it started.

If we held on after JDSU started falling, we wouldn't have made a dime. But we had the courage to let it ride. We had the courage to get rich. **We had our trailing stop strategy in place and the discipline to follow it and get out**.

Of course, they don't all work out like this. And you can vary the strategy, like tightening up the stop so you don't have as much downside risk. But the point remains...

When one of the world's smartest investors thanks me for a tip I gave him that has made him a lot of money, it's probably worth sharing with you.

You've got to have the courage to be right... to let your good calls ride. As I said to Rick a few years ago...

You never know how high an asset's price can soar... so you can simply use a mental trailing stop to both protect yourself and, more importantly, get out at a much higher price.

The courage to be rich... to let a big winner ride... is just as important as the courage to be right in this game.

Chapter 26

Supreme Investing Confidence: How I Got It and How You Can, Too

Published November 27, 2009

"Why did it take me until age 38 to get here?" I asked my wife.

She said, *"At least it didn't take you until age 68. And really, most people never get there."*

I'm talking about total confidence... total conviction in your investments.

That doesn't mean being cocky or being foolish or taking big risks. It means having the certainty to invest when the time is right.

Look, I know I'm the same knucklehead I was a decade ago... I haven't picked up any significant new skills. But I do have something far more valuable when it comes to investing: I have conviction. And it's paid off, as I'll explain.

A decade ago, though I was relatively young, I had plenty of experience. I had completed my PhD... I'd been the vice president of a global mutual fund... and I'd written an investment newsletter for a few years.

But when it came to my own investments, I didn't do as well as I could have. **It's because I listened to others**...

Fifteen years ago, I'd share what I thought was a unique idea with someone superior to me at work, and they'd knock it down. Since I thought it was a good idea, I'd share it with someone else. They'd knock it down, too. I'd keep going, with the same results.

When everyone above you says your idea stinks, it probably stinks, right? That's what I thought back then... And that is true in most of life.

But that is NOT true in investing.

Once I stopped caring what others thought, I started making real money.

Here are a few things I've done with conviction in the last decade...

- In January 2000, when most people were crazy for stocks, I wrote in my newsletter: "*We are at the peak of most likely the greatest financial mania that will ever be seen.*" The Nasdaq fell 75% peak to trough in just over three years.

- In 2003, I started investing in and writing about gold. I've never had more people tell me my idea stinks or look at me like I'm crazy than when I wrote about gold. But gold went from a low near $250 in 2001 to near $1,200 today. [*Editor's note: Gold soared up to a high of about $1,900 per ounce in 2011 before falling back to around $1,300 in 2017.*]

- In March 2009, when everyone thought the world was going to end, I personally invested a big stake of money in stocks – my biggest speculation ever. I closed out that big speculation in June 2009, for a large profit.

Lately, I've been buying extremely depressed Florida real estate. Friends and family are asking why. They won't say it, but they think it's foolish... that it's dead money... that it won't come back for a while.

For the first time ever, their opinions don't even faze me. Honestly, the prices I'm paying... jeez... Nowadays, you can buy trophy properties out of your checkbook.

So please, call me foolish. The more I'm called a fool, the more I have conviction I'm right.

If you've done your homework and you believe you're right, it's OK to ask everyone to punch holes in your idea. That's what you SHOULD do. The trick is to separate FACTS from OPINIONS. When the facts and opinions don't line up – bingo. It's time to buy.

The true liberation for me... the true ability to make really big profits... came when – after I'd done my homework and most smart people *still* disagreed with me – I was bold enough to step up and make the investment anyway.

I only kick myself a bit because I could have done this years ago. But my wife is right. Better to get it at 38 than at 68... or never.

The nice part from here is, I know that every few years, I will find a special opportunity... and I will have the conviction to jump on it when the time is right.

I hope you can get there too. Have courage. Have conviction. Dot all your *I*s and cross all your *T*s, of course. But take the leap!

Chapter 27

My Best 'How to Get Rich' Advice

Published May 29, 2013

I've just hired a new employee...

He's young – 22 years old. But I've known him since he was 10, when he lived two doors down from me. And I want to get him pointed in the right direction in life... right now.

What advice do you give a 22-year-old just starting out? It's the same advice I'd give just about anyone who wants to grow his wealth...

I quickly pulled the book *How to Get Rich* by Felix Dennis off my bookshelf. This book is fantastic for my new employee... and maybe you, too.

How to Get Rich **is the most honest story of how to generate wealth I've ever read**.

The book isn't like any other "self-help" book you've ever read. It's a rare gem for two reasons...

1. It was written by a guy who actually made himself filthy rich.

2. The guy can write. It is an easy read.

As for advice for the young man in my office, Dennis writes:

> If you are young, then I ask to you remember just this: You are richer than anyone older than you... Time is always running on, and the young have more of it in their pocket than the richest man or woman alive...

Continuing on this idea, if you could *"turn the clock back for me by 40 years,"* Dennis says, *"I would willingly swap you every penny and every possession I own in return. And I would have the better end of the bargain, too!"*

The young are richer than the richest man... I love that perspective for a young man starting out.

But the book is not just about advice for young people starting out – far from it. It's for all people aspiring to have more money in their lives.

I guarantee you will disagree with Dennis on many things that he says. You won't believe that rich people think the way he does... or that what he says is really how to get rich. But from what I've learned after accumulating a few dollars in my life, Felix Dennis is telling the truth.

Don't get me wrong... the book is not a step-by-step how-to guide on getting rich. But to me, it is far more valuable. *It is an accurate explanation of how Dennis became rich and what he thinks it would take for you to get rich, too.*

He dares you to make yourself rich... to go for it. And he warns you will never get rich if...

- You are unwilling to fail.

- You care what the neighbors think.

- You are not prepared to work longer hours than almost anyone you know.

- You cannot convince yourself that you are "good enough" to be rich.

Felix Dennis doesn't sugarcoat it. He tells it how it is.

It is a must-read for my new young employee... And going back through it this week reminded me that it's a must-read for you, too.

– Chapter 28 –

Investment Advice TO a World Champ

January 13, 2015

I met a legend... a now-retired international sports hero.

I don't want to share his name because he told me quietly that he could use some financial help, and he probably wouldn't want that word out in public.

I didn't answer him when we were together. But as I thought about it later, the right advice for him is the same advice that I would give to you...

This is serious stuff. I urge you to take it seriously, and commit these ideas to memory. Let's get started:

1. **Nobody will care more about your finances than you.**

This is critical for you to embrace, immediately. Nobody is going to care more about your finances than you. You simply can't just find somebody smart and hand your money responsibilities off to them.

You can't just hand off your life and hope it goes okay – *this is your life we're talking about*! How many rock stars and sports stars have you read about that are broke today because they handed off this responsibility? Don't do it.

The quicker you take control and ultimate responsibility with your money, the quicker you will start building your legitimate fortune. And you can't ever give up that responsibility.

Let me be clear... It is alright – even smart – to work with smart people, and to delegate some of your money responsibilities to carefully chosen people. The important part is, you just can't "check out." You have to be the team captain here... the captain of your money ship.

2. **There is no magic bullet, or shortcut**.

You didn't become a sports legend by taking shortcuts. You had to work harder than the next guy, learn more than him, and focus with more intensity than the next guy to achieve your goals.

If you want to invest successfully, you have to do the same thing. You can't get by on one hot tip after another. The shortcuts don't work. This leads us to the third idea...

3. **If you don't understand it, don't buy it**.

It's easy to get dazzled by promises of big profits... It's even easier to get sucked in when the promises are accompanied by slick brochures and fast talk with a lot of words that you don't understand.

You'll save yourself a lot of loss (and time) if you remember this: If you don't understand it, don't buy it. Don't ever cheat on this one. It will cost you.

4. **Buy investments that are 1) cheap, 2) hated, AND 3) in an uptrend**.

I've built my wealth and reputation on this philosophy. In short, you can't buy what's already incredibly popular – because if you do, chances are you've already missed it. Instead, you have to buy what people are skeptical of.

Separately, waiting for an uptrend is a crucial part of this strategy as well... It helps take the risk out of the idea, and it helps "confirm" that your investment thesis is "right."

If you want my opinion today, property is probably your best bet.

Here's why:

It's *surprisingly* affordable (when you factor in today's record-low interest rates). I say "surprisingly" because most people look at house prices versus incomes, and they wrongly assume that house prices are expensive. The correct way to look at it is relative to monthly payments (interest rates). And based on that, house prices are plenty affordable after all.

Also, investors are skeptical about property now, wrongly thinking that it is overpriced. (So it is hated – or at least not loved). AND property is in an uptrend. PERFECT.

Best of all, you can understand it. You hold the keys, you paint the walls... with YOUR property, you control your destiny.

My money is where my mouth is with this one... Back in 2010, I owned no property outside of my home. Today, property makes up the biggest percentage of my own financial assets – by far.

Property is what I'm doing with my own money.

You will always hear about ways to make higher returns, or faster ways to make a buck, than property. But chances are today you'd be risking much more than you can imagine, relative to the potential reward. It's simply not worth it.

Again, property is affordable, unloved, in an uptrend, and understandable. You control your destiny, to a better degree than with other investments. Particularly if you are not an expert in investing, and don't intend to be, then property makes sense for you.

I could go on and on about "do's" and "don'ts" when it comes to your money... But I won't.

Instead, let's leave it at these simple-but-absolutely-critical points...

1. Nobody will care more about your situation than you, so don't hand off your finances.

2. There is no magic bullet or shortcut. (The "hot tip" doesn't exist.)

3. If you don't understand it, don't buy it. (If it sounds too good to be true, it probably is.)

4. Buy investments that are cheap, hated, and that have started their uptrend.

That's it. Commit these points to memory and you are that much closer to living richly and investing wisely.

Further Reading
From Our Friends at Stansberry Research

You can pick up any of these titles at Amazon.com.

From Porter Stansberry

America 2020: The Survival Blueprint

America 2020 Volume II: How the Richest Men in America Are Protecting Their Wealth Right Now

America 2020: The New Crisis

From Dr. David Eifrig, Jr.

Dr. David Eifrig Jr.'s Big Book of Retirement Secrets

The Doctor's Protocol Field Manual

High Income Retirement

The Living Cure: The Promise of Cancer Immunotherapy

From Dan Ferris

World Dominating Dividend Growers: Income Streams That Never Go Down

From the Stansberry Research Team

The Stansberry Research Starter's Guide

The Stansberry Research Guide to Investment Basics

The World's Greatest Investment Ideas

Dividend Millionaire